AF703234

The 24-Hour Martial Arts Story with ChatGPT

Andrew Parry

Published by Andrew Parry, 2025.

While every precaution has been taken in the preparation of this book, the publisher assumes no responsibility for errors or omissions, or for damages resulting from the use of the information contained herein.

THE 24-HOUR MARTIAL ARTS STORY WITH CHATGPT

First edition. April 25, 2025.

Copyright © 2025 Andrew Parry.

ISBN: 979-8231930166

Written by Andrew Parry.

Table of Contents

Why Martial Arts Stories Still Kick Ass

There's something undeniably timeless about a martial arts story. No matter how many times we've seen a hero rise from humble beginnings to face off against a powerful rival, it never loses its grip. From ancient legends to modern films and series, the martial arts narrative keeps coming back stronger, faster, and more emotionally impactful. And it's not just the flying kicks or slow-motion punches that hook us. It's what those moves *mean*. Martial arts stories are packed with themes of honor, discipline, self-control, legacy, revenge, redemption, and often, a deeper search for identity. They speak to something primal in all of us—the desire to overcome our weaknesses and become more than we are.

The genre has a unique way of blending philosophy and action. One moment you're watching or reading about a brutal street fight, and the next you're meditating with the hero beneath a waterfall, questioning your place in the universe. That balance between external action and internal transformation is what makes martial arts stories stand out. They're not just about beating someone up. They're about beating the odds, conquering the self, and fighting for something that matters. And that fight can happen in a tournament ring, a war-torn village, a futuristic dojo, or even within the mind.

Audiences love a good underdog. That's why martial arts protagonists are often nobodies at the beginning. The janitor who sweeps the mats but secretly practices. The bullied kid who stumbles upon an old master. The ex-soldier trying to find peace in a violent world. These aren't superheroes with lasers and tech suits. These are characters we can relate to. Their power comes not from magic or money, but from relentless training and unbreakable spirit. And that makes their victories so satisfying. When they finally land that finishing blow on the arrogant champion or the corrupt crime boss, we cheer because it feels *earned*.

Another reason martial arts stories stay relevant is their visual and emotional storytelling. Fights in these stories aren't random scuffles—they're turning points. Every punch carries weight. Every block, every dodge, every stance tells us something about who the character is at that moment. Is the hero still holding back out of fear or mercy? Is the villain fighting from anger or desperation? Combat becomes a kind of dance, a language. And when written well, it's just as powerful on the page as it is on the screen. That's where writing with ChatGPT comes in handy. You can ask it to help choreograph a fight based on your characters' personalities, their goals, their strengths and weaknesses. You're not just describing kicks—you're telling a story through movement.

The genre is also incredibly flexible. You can write a martial arts story in almost any setting or time period. Historical samurai tale? Absolutely. Sci-fi ninja warriors in space? Sure thing. Underground MMA tournament in a dystopian future? Go wild. Martial arts fiction can carry drama, comedy, tragedy, horror, and even romance. It's a genre chameleon, which means your creativity has room to stretch without leaving the fighting spirit behind. And because these stories have global roots—from Chinese kung fu to Japanese jujutsu, from Thai Muay Thai to Brazilian capoeira—you have a treasure trove of culture, tradition, and style to explore and honor in your writing.

On a deeper level, martial arts stories also appeal to something psychological. They often explore control in a chaotic world. The hero learns to discipline the body to master the mind. In a time when everything around us feels unstable or unpredictable, the martial arts story offers a kind of promise: you can shape your fate with enough effort. That message is both inspiring and empowering, especially when delivered through a compelling character journey. When we see a fighter who used to lose control of their temper learn to fight with calm precision, or a student who was afraid of confrontation finally stand up to injustice, it hits hard—because we recognize that struggle in ourselves.

Let's not forget the cool factor, either. Martial arts stories are *fun*. They're fast-paced, visually dynamic, and loaded with satisfying reversals. A good fight scene is like a puzzle being solved in real time. And when a hero pulls off a move we saw them fail to execute in an earlier scene, it creates a narrative payoff that feels like a standing ovation moment. That's something you can build toward even in a short story or one-day screenplay draft. All you need is a character who wants something, a reason they can't have it, an opponent in the way, and a training journey that changes them by the time they return for the final battle.

With ChatGPT, you can quickly brainstorm the world, characters, and story beats of a martial arts tale. You don't have to get bogged down trying to name a dojo or decide if your hero should specialize in Wing Chun or Jeet Kune Do. You can just ask. You can test out different story setups in seconds—maybe your hero is an undercover cop in a martial arts cult, or maybe they're trying to win a tournament to pay for a sibling's surgery. The possibilities multiply, but you'll never be overwhelmed because the tool helps you focus on momentum.

What's more, you can experiment without fear. Want to mash up wuxia fantasy with cyberpunk? Go for it. Want to do a quiet, introspective story about an old master training their last student before dying? That works too. You can try bold ideas quickly and keep what works. Martial arts fiction thrives on emotion and energy, and writing with AI lets you tap into both without the drag of second-guessing every word.

This book is going to show you how to do all of that—build compelling martial arts stories fast, confidently, and with enough emotional and narrative punch to hit your readers right in the heart. By the end of it, you'll not only have written a complete story, but you'll also understand the heartbeat of martial arts fiction and how to keep it alive in whatever tale you choose to tell next.

Because let's face it—martial arts stories still kick ass. And so will yours.

Finding the Core Idea That Punches Through

Every great martial arts story begins with a single punch—not a literal one, but a thematic strike that hits deep. The core idea is the heartbeat of your entire narrative. It's what gives your story weight, purpose, and drive. It's what separates a bland sequence of kicks and punches from a tale that resonates and lingers. Whether you're writing a novel, short story, or screenplay, that central concept needs to be powerful enough to carry your entire project. And the beauty of working with ChatGPT is that you can explore dozens of core ideas in minutes until you find the one that connects with your creative pulse.

So what exactly *is* a core idea? It's not the setting or the main fight scene. It's the soul of the story, the emotional engine that everything else revolves around. Think of it as the "why" behind all the action. Why is this character fighting? Why does this story need to be told? Why should anyone care? When you nail that idea, every plot point, every character interaction, and every fight suddenly has meaning. You're not just throwing fists into the air—you're delivering a message that lands.

Let's say your core idea is about *redemption*. Maybe your protagonist is a former gang enforcer who's trying to walk the peaceful path but is dragged back into violence to protect someone they love. Or maybe your core idea is *revenge*, but you flip it and make it about how revenge poisons the one who seeks it. These are powerful concepts, and they don't need to be complicated. In fact, the simpler and cleaner the core idea, the more direct and emotional the story becomes.

When brainstorming with ChatGPT, you can start by testing a few of these core ideas. Try typing something like, "Give me five emotionally compelling core ideas for a martial arts story," or "What are some martial arts story themes that center around forgiveness or identity?" What comes back might surprise you. You could end up with a tale about a young fighter who must choose between winning a tournament for glory or throwing the match to save a friend. Or a wandering martial artist who's sworn never to fight again—until injustice forces their hand. The possibilities are endless, but the key is to pick one that makes *you* feel something. If you feel it, chances are your reader will too.

A strong core idea also helps keep your story focused. When you've only got a day to write, every scene needs to serve the heart of the story. There's no room for filler. With your idea in place, you can always ask yourself, "Does this moment support the core theme?" If it doesn't, you can rewrite or remove it without hesitation. This is how you maintain clarity and momentum. Whether you're writing a slow-burn emotional arc or an action-packed showdown, that core idea is the throughline that guides every decision.

It also gives you a foundation for the protagonist's journey. A story about honor might show a young fighter learning that winning isn't everything. A story about legacy might follow a reluctant student who must carry on their fallen master's teachings. These ideas shape who your characters are, what they care about, and how they grow. Without that center, the coolest fights in the world won't mean anything. But when the final battle ties back to what the story is really *about*, it lands like a knockout blow.

Don't worry if you're not sure what your core idea is at first. That's what ChatGPT is for. You can ask it to help you distill your loose ideas into something tight and clear. If you start with a vague pitch like "A street fighter enters a tournament," you can ask, "What deeper emotional theme could anchor this story?" You might discover it's about proving self-worth without violence. Or maybe it's about reconciling with a father who trained the villain. Suddenly, the fights aren't just fights—they're a conversation, a confrontation, a crucible.

You can also work backwards. Maybe you already have a scene in your head—a brutal alley fight, a tearful reunion in a dojo, a tense moment before the final round. Ask yourself what that scene is really *saying*. Is it about fear? Control? Freedom? Often, your story already knows what it wants to say—you just need to listen.

Here's a tip: try to describe your story idea in a single sentence that includes the emotional core. Not "A guy trains to win a tournament," but "A grieving son enters a brutal underground tournament to avenge his brother, only to discover that forgiveness is stronger than vengeance." That's an idea that punches through. That's something readers can latch onto. And it gives you direction the whole way through.

The genre gives you a lot of room to move, so don't be afraid to pick a bold idea. You could go mythical or futuristic, grounded or spiritual. But no matter the setting or style, the human core stays the same. It's always about struggle. It's always about growth. It's always about facing something that hurts and deciding who you are when the fight ends.

In the next chapters, we'll dive into how to build the story structure around that idea, how to choose characters who reflect and challenge it, and how to choreograph fights that feel personal and powerful. But none of that matters without a strong center.

So take a moment. Let your imagination explore. Talk it through with ChatGPT. Don't settle for just "cool"—find the idea that *means* something to you. That's when you'll know it's the one that punches through.

Writing Backwards From the Final Fight

One of the fastest ways to write a powerful martial arts story is to start with the climax—the final fight. That scene, when your hero faces their greatest opponent, is the destination your whole story is traveling toward. It's not just a battle of fists and feet. It's an emotional payoff. It's the test of everything the character has learned. If you can picture that scene clearly, everything else becomes a series of stepping stones leading up to it. Writing backwards from the final fight isn't just a time-saving trick—it's a strategy that ensures your story lands with force.

Think of it like building a path through the jungle. If you start hacking away from the beginning, you might get lost. But if you know exactly where you want to end up, every step gets you closer. With ChatGPT, this approach becomes even more useful because once you describe your final confrontation, you can use the AI to help you reverse engineer all the scenes that need to happen to make that moment hit like a finishing blow.

So how do you design a final fight worth writing toward? It starts with stakes. What's on the line? It could be life or death, honor, a student's future, a family's redemption, or the soul of a dojo. Whatever it is, it has to matter deeply to your protagonist. And it needs to represent the culmination of their emotional journey. If your hero started the story angry and impulsive, this fight should test their ability to stay calm and focused. If they started off as someone running from their past, this is the moment they stop and face it head-on. The fight itself becomes a metaphor for who they've become.

This is the scene where the theme of your story becomes physical. If your story is about control, then maybe the villain tries to provoke the hero into a rage—but the hero wins by staying centered. If the story is about legacy, the fight might echo moves taught by a fallen master. This is the moment where all the training, all the setbacks, all the pain comes together. So picture it. Where does it take place? What's the atmosphere? Is it a quiet forest clearing under the moonlight, a roaring stadium packed with bloodthirsty fans, or a crumbling temple in a rainstorm? Your setting will enhance the emotional stakes.

Once you know what the final confrontation looks and feels like, start moving backwards. What needed to happen just before this? Maybe the hero almost didn't show up. Maybe they made peace with someone important. Maybe they learned a secret about the villain's weakness. Now go a step earlier. What pushed them to that point? What was their lowest moment? You're working in reverse like a fight choreographer running the tape backward to understand every movement.

Let's say your final fight is between the hero and their former best friend, now turned enemy. You already have emotion baked in. So ask: what caused their friendship to break? When did it happen? What was the betrayal? Did the hero try to reconcile before the final confrontation? These questions become scenes. ChatGPT can help you outline the fallout from that broken relationship, scenes that build tension, and moments of foreshadowing so when the final fight comes, it feels inevitable.

Writing backwards also helps you avoid filler. Every scene must push the character toward the climax. If a moment doesn't contribute to the final fight—either by building tension, advancing the theme, or showing character growth—it's probably unnecessary. This keeps your story lean, powerful, and emotionally loaded. It also helps with pacing. Martial arts stories are known for their balance of stillness and action, and this approach ensures each fight, each pause, and each training scene has a clear purpose.

Another benefit of working backward is the clarity it gives your protagonist's arc. You know where they'll be emotionally and physically at the end, so you can map out how they evolve to reach that point. If your final scene shows them using a technique they once failed at, you know you need a scene early in the story where they try and fail. If the climax hinges on inner peace, show them being reckless or aggressive early on. Now their journey has a shape—a direction that flows toward transformation.

ChatGPT can be a huge help in building that reverse-engineered structure. Try prompting it with something like, "Given this final fight scene, what are the key emotional and plot beats that need to happen before it to make the ending satisfying?" It will suggest training sequences, moments of doubt, character relationships, mentor advice, rival confrontations—all the story ingredients that organically lead to your destination. Then you can arrange those beats like a ladder the character must climb.

Let's not forget that the final fight is also where the reader or viewer feels the biggest catharsis. That doesn't happen by accident. It happens when every choice made earlier in the story builds pressure that releases in that one explosive moment. When your hero finally defeats the antagonist—not just physically, but morally or emotionally—it feels like justice, or peace, or personal triumph. Writing backwards gives you the tools to plan that build-up with precision.

Even if you're writing fast, this approach keeps you from losing your narrative thread. You're no longer trying to come up with what happens next. You're filling in the necessary steps to get to what already exists. It frees you to be creative within structure. You can still add twists, humor, romance, or tragedy—but always with the awareness that it's all in service of that final showdown.

So before you write your first page, spend some time writing your last scene. Visualize the fight. Hear the dialogue. Feel the emotions. Know the outcome. Then start asking yourself: what had to happen to make this moment possible? Let ChatGPT help you sketch out the path in reverse. That way, when you start writing forward, you'll move with speed and purpose. No wasted effort. No detours. Just a direct line to the moment that matters most.

That's how you write with impact. That's how you keep your story tight. And that's how you make sure your final fight hits hard—and never misses.

Creating a Structure Built for Showdowns

The martial arts story thrives on rhythm. It's not just a series of fights thrown together like highlights on a reel—it's a journey with rising stakes, shifting emotions, and a final, climactic battle that feels earned. To pull that off in a single day, you need a structure that serves your showdown from beginning to end. You're not just building a story—you're building a runway. And the showdown is the takeoff. Everything else, from training sequences to personal revelations, leads us toward that moment when your hero finally steps into the ring, alleyway, temple courtyard, or whatever battleground you've chosen.

Martial arts stories often follow the classic three-act structure, which gives your narrative a spine. But this isn't some rigid blueprint—it's a flexible framework that can be tailored to your specific character arc and the kind of fights you want to showcase. When you think of your story like a series of escalating challenges and emotional shifts, everything falls into place naturally. And with ChatGPT, once you plug in your idea and final fight, the AI can help you fill in those structural beats so you're not stuck figuring it out along the way.

In Act One, you introduce your fighter and the world they live in. This is the quiet before the storm—or at least the build-up before the first jab lands. We need to see what your hero lacks. Maybe they're cocky and need humility. Maybe they're broken and need purpose. Maybe they're hiding from violence and have to be drawn back into it. This act usually ends with a call to action, a challenge thrown, or a major defeat that sets the story in motion. The point is to show that the hero is not yet ready for the final fight. They have the potential, sure—but they haven't earned it.

In Act Two, the pressure mounts. This is the training arc, the rivalries heating up, the self-doubt creeping in. It's where the hero starts to transform, physically and emotionally. It's also where most of your smaller showdowns live—sparring matches, street fights, dojo duels, ambushes in alleys. These fights aren't just cool moments (though they can be visually awesome). They're all building character. Maybe your hero wins but in a dishonorable way. Maybe they lose and learn something critical. Each fight escalates the stakes and teaches a lesson. If you're writing fast, you can ask ChatGPT to suggest fight scenes that reveal personality traits or reflect inner conflict. The more your fights tie into the story's heart, the more powerful they'll be.

This second act often includes what feels like the lowest point. Maybe the hero walks away from fighting. Maybe their master dies. Maybe they lose a friend or get betrayed. Whatever it is, it shakes them to the core. This moment clears the way for transformation. It's the emotional breaking point that makes the final act necessary. And if you're writing with the final showdown in mind, you'll know exactly what kind of growth your character needs to undergo between here and there.

Then comes Act Three—the climb back, the rising tension, and the final confrontation. This is where your hero steps into the arena not just with stronger fists, but a clearer heart. The theme of your story comes alive in their choices, in their tactics, in their restraint or ferocity. It's not just about winning—it's about becoming. The final fight should echo all the earlier conflicts but push further. It should reflect who your hero is *now*, versus who they were when they started.

Let's break this structure down even more simply so you can hit it fast when writing with ChatGPT. You could phrase your request like: "Give me a martial arts story outline with a reluctant hero, an emotional loss in the middle, and a redemptive final fight." Or: "Build me a three-act structure with a street-level setting, an internal conflict about identity, and a final battle against a former mentor." You'll get something tight and usable, which you can then customize with your own twists and ideas.

The key thing is momentum. Your structure should feel like it's always moving forward—even when the hero pauses to reflect or question everything. Every scene should either introduce a new challenge, deepen a relationship, or set up the next emotional hit. Martial arts stories are powered by progression. Not just physical, but moral and spiritual. So structure your fights and story arcs in a way that clearly tracks that evolution.

Another great approach is to think of your story as a sequence of fights, each one bigger or deeper than the last. The first might be a casual sparring session. The next could be a rough street brawl with real consequences. Then comes the emotional fight—a battle that forces the hero to confront something internal. Maybe it's against a loved one, a mentor, or someone they don't want to hurt. These stages create a rhythm that makes the final fight feel like the peak. You can even label your fights when planning: First Test, Emotional Clash, Breaking Point, Final Reckoning. It gives you a map. A structure that ensures each showdown hits harder than the last.

Your story doesn't have to be long to be impactful. In fact, short and sharp can be even more powerful in martial arts fiction. Readers want to *feel* something when the final kick lands. They want to know that it mattered. So when building your structure, make every punch count. Use ChatGPT to help refine pacing, fill in any slow stretches, and make sure your emotional beats match your physical ones.

By the time you reach the final act, you want the reader to be holding their breath. Not because the fight might be lost, but because the hero might not walk away unchanged. That's what makes a showdown matter. That's what gives your story punch. So build your structure like a staircase, every step a little higher, a little harder, until there's nowhere left to go but forward into the fight that will define everything.

The Three-Act Journey of the Warrior

There's something classic and unshakably strong about the three-act structure when it comes to martial arts storytelling. It's not just because it works—it's because it mirrors the warrior's transformation. The rise, the fall, the return. Beginning, middle, end. It's not just about pacing your story for readability or for screen structure—it's about following the natural rhythm of growth that any fighter, real or fictional, must pass through to earn their moment of victory. When you're trying to write a complete martial arts narrative in a single day, wrapping it around a solid three-act backbone is one of the best things you can do to keep your energy focused and your story emotionally rich.

Act One is all about who your warrior is before the world pushes them to change. It's the moment in the story where we meet your protagonist in a state of imbalance—whether they know it or not. Maybe they're already a fighter, full of ego and untamed power. Maybe they've sworn off violence entirely, living in the shadow of something they once did or failed to do. Or maybe they're a total rookie, unaware of their potential and living far from the world of martial conflict. Whatever the case, this is the setup. You show us their environment, their relationships, and most importantly, the internal struggle they may not be ready to face. This act usually ends with what we might call the "first confrontation"—a moment when the world kicks in the door, throws a challenge at your hero, and demands a response.

Act Two is the war zone of transformation. It's where the warrior gets pushed, broken, and shaped. In this act, your hero often agrees to take on the challenge—or gets dragged into it—but is still far from being ready. This is the act of training, learning, stumbling, failing, and changing. The battles here are both external and internal. Maybe there's a powerful rival constantly one step ahead. Maybe the hero's own emotions get in the way: fear, rage, grief, doubt. This is the part of the journey where the warrior becomes *worthy* of the final fight—not just by building muscle or mastering moves, but by confronting what's really holding them back. This act almost always includes a pivotal low point—a defeat so devastating, physical or emotional, that the hero questions everything.

What makes Act Two so juicy in martial arts stories is the layering. Yes, you can have incredible fight scenes here, but they have to *mean* something. A tournament match that shows your hero isn't ready. A training session that reveals an emotional block. A confrontation with an ally that puts their philosophy to the test. These are more than cool action beats—they're growth moments. And the second act gives you all the space to show that growth slowly and powerfully. With ChatGPT, you can create this arc by simply saying, "What are five scenes that show my martial arts hero struggling to control their anger during training?" Boom—you've got a meaningful second act coming together fast.

Then comes Act Three, where the warrior emerges transformed. Not perfect. Not invincible. But ready. This is where the tension peaks, the stakes are clear, and the final confrontation looms. If Act One is about who they were, and Act Two is about who they're becoming, then Act Three is the payoff—it's about who they've *decided* to be. And that decision gets tested, usually through one final, emotionally loaded showdown. This fight is never just physical. Maybe the hero is trying to win without crossing a moral line. Maybe they're trying to protect someone rather than punish someone. Maybe they're facing a mirror version of who they used to be. The key is that the final act feels like a resolution—not just of plot, but of identity.

This act can also bring surprising reversals. Maybe the enemy turns out to be someone the hero must save. Maybe the real antagonist is revealed only after the final fight. Martial arts stories allow for this kind of twist because they're deeply personal. They're not always about beating the villain—they're about beating the part of yourself that wants to give up, give in, or lash out. That's what audiences remember. That's why these stories linger.

So how do you use ChatGPT to plan your three-act structure fast? Easy. Once you've got your core idea and final fight in mind, just ask: "Help me build a three-act story about a disgraced fighter who must train a student to win a tournament," or "Give me a three-act structure for a martial arts story about revenge that becomes forgiveness." The AI will give you a clean outline—your Act One setup, Act Two trials, Act Three payoff—and you can start writing scenes right away. You'll know what your hero needs to feel, learn, and face in each section.

Here's the real magic of using the three-act structure in a martial arts narrative: it mimics the movements of a fight. The first act is the stance. It's preparation, breathing, awareness. The second act is the clash. The give and take, the pain, the fury, the strategy. The third act is the strike. The final move, executed with everything the fighter has learned, all building to that single, defining moment. It's elegant. It's timeless. And when done right, it's unforgettable.

So don't stress about inventing something revolutionary. Structure isn't your enemy—it's your ally. When you've only got a day to write, this framework helps you stay grounded and intentional. It lets your creativity move freely, because you know the path. You know when to pause, when to escalate, and when to hit hard. And with ChatGPT backing you up, you're never more than a sentence away from getting the next piece of the journey in place.

The warrior's path is always threefold—beginning, test, transformation. And whether your hero is a monk, a mercenary, or a misfit, that journey remains the same. That's what makes martial arts stories powerful. That's what makes them last. And that's what will make yours one worth remembering.

Mapping the Hero's Path in Martial Arts Fiction

Every martial arts story is, at its heart, a personal transformation. The hero doesn't just learn to punch harder or kick faster—they evolve, break, heal, and become someone new. That journey is what makes the story compelling. The best martial arts tales are never just about fighting. They're about *why* the hero fights, what changes inside them, and how they carry that change through to the final moment. So when we talk about mapping the hero's path in martial arts fiction, we're talking about more than just plot points. We're talking about the emotional and philosophical journey that gives every strike meaning.

The classic "Hero's Journey," with all its mythic beats, fits martial arts stories perfectly. You've probably seen it in a hundred different forms: the call to action, the reluctant student, the wise master, the brutal training, the moment of failure, the rebirth, and finally the ultimate confrontation. But you don't need to follow every step like it's a checklist. Instead, use it like a compass to guide your character through the narrative wilderness. You can ask ChatGPT to build this path for you, tailored to the type of story you're telling. Whether you're writing a short story or a feature-length screenplay, the bones of this journey will hold strong.

So let's break it down into stages you can use and remix as needed.

The path begins in the ordinary world. Your hero is either unaware of their potential, actively avoiding it, or stuck in a life that doesn't reflect who they really are. This could be a street kid in a city ruled by gangs, a former martial artist who's hung up the gloves, or someone who's just never fought before but holds a quiet fire inside. This part of the story is about emotional restlessness. Your hero doesn't quite belong, even if they think they do.

Then comes the call to action. Something happens that pulls them toward conflict. A rival shows up. A loved one is hurt. A tournament is announced. A master appears with a challenge. Whatever it is, it disturbs the balance of your hero's world. They're pushed into action—usually reluctantly. Martial arts heroes are often driven by duty, guilt, or necessity rather than ambition. That hesitation is part of what makes them feel real.

Early on, the hero meets a mentor or teacher—sometimes traditional, sometimes not. This figure doesn't just teach technique—they pass on a worldview. This is where you bring in the philosophy of your martial arts style. Is it about balance? Respect? Power through control? Your master character should be the living embodiment of that ideal. And your hero must struggle with it, misinterpret it, reject it, and ultimately grow into it. The hero's path isn't about accepting wisdom—it's about earning it.

The middle part of the journey is full of trials—physical, emotional, and relational. Your hero might be training in secret. They might be clashing with a rival. They might be questioning whether they have what it takes. This is where internal conflict really ramps up. In many martial arts stories, the hero's biggest opponent is *themselves*. Their fear. Their anger. Their past. Their ego. And the fights they have along the way aren't just about defeating others—they're about facing these inner obstacles and beginning to change.

Eventually, they hit a low point. They lose a match. They're betrayed. Their teacher dies. They break their code. Something happens that strips them down completely. It's painful. Humbling. But it's also necessary. Because after that comes the moment of clarity—the scene where the hero remembers why they're fighting, who they want to become, and what it will cost to get there. This is the emotional turning point, the place where all the lessons and losses finally take root.

Now the path leads toward the final confrontation. But this time, your hero walks it with purpose. They're not perfect. They're not invincible. But they've changed. They've integrated the wisdom. They've mastered themselves. And that mastery becomes visible in how they fight—not just in skill, but in restraint, strategy, or self-sacrifice. The final fight is a mirror, reflecting who the hero used to be and who they've become. If you've mapped the path clearly, that moment will be electric, because it's not just about fists. It's about fulfillment.

When you're writing fast, as in a single-day project, having this emotional map is everything. It keeps your story grounded and gives every scene weight. You don't need to write all the beats in exact order—you can use ChatGPT to help outline or expand any section. For example, you might say, "Give me three scenes that show my martial arts hero failing to live up to their teacher's code," or "Describe an emotional turning point where the student realizes the true meaning of martial arts." You'll get responses that you can reshape into dialogue, internal reflection, or action sequences.

Also, remember that this path doesn't need to be grand or dramatic to be meaningful. Even a small-scale story—one about a teenager learning to stand up for themselves, or a single mother finding strength through community dojo training—can carry the same arc. The stakes don't have to be global. They just have to be *personal.* And that's where martial arts fiction shines. The personal journey becomes universal. The private fight becomes everyone's.

You might even want to sketch the hero's path visually. Draw a line, mark the key moments: the call, the teacher, the trials, the breaking point, the return, the fight. Then you can fill in scenes around those beats as you write. Ask ChatGPT to help brainstorm each section. "What should my character learn in their first defeat?" or "How can I show the hero beginning to change during a training session?" The answers come quickly, and you stay focused on forward movement.

At the end of the day, mapping the hero's path in martial arts fiction is about honoring the transformation. The fights are cool, the settings can be epic, and the choreography might sparkle—but it's the internal arc that readers or viewers carry with them long after the final blow. That's what elevates your story from action to art.

So think about who your hero is at the start—and who they must become to win the final fight. Trace that journey step by step. Build your story around that evolution. And with the help of ChatGPT, keep your creative process moving as swiftly and decisively as a master's strike.

Designing the Ultimate Showdown First

If there's one thing every reader or viewer remembers in a martial arts story, it's the final fight. The ultimate showdown. The clash that defines everything—the stakes, the emotions, the transformation of the hero. Designing this moment first is one of the smartest moves you can make when writing a martial arts narrative, especially when you're working fast. It gives you direction, purpose, and most importantly, *impact*. Once you know how the story ends, everything that comes before can be reverse-engineered to support it. You don't just end strong—you build toward it with precision and momentum.

Let's start with what makes a final showdown unforgettable. It's not just the choreography or location, though both can elevate the scene. What truly gives this moment weight is what it represents. The fight isn't just about who wins—it's about *what* gets resolved. Emotionally. Philosophically. Spiritually. The ultimate showdown isn't just fists flying—it's truth versus lies, growth versus stagnation, peace versus chaos. So before you think about punches, think about purpose. What does your protagonist need to prove, accept, or reject in this final moment? What is at stake beyond the belt or the title or the vengeance?

Once you answer that, you can begin to sculpt the moment visually and emotionally. Ask yourself: where does the showdown take place? Location matters in martial arts stories. It becomes a character in the scene. Is it a moonlit rooftop in the city? A rain-soaked jungle temple? A tournament ring surrounded by thousands? A quiet dojo with only echoes for company? The setting should mirror the theme. A chaotic environment can reflect the character's internal turmoil. A serene one can highlight the tension that exists in stillness. Whatever you choose, let it enhance what the fight means, not just what it looks like.

Now think about the opponent. This isn't just someone to beat. This is the final test. The antagonist needs to challenge the hero on more than just a physical level. They should represent something that the hero has struggled with—an ideology, a fear, a personal flaw. Maybe they were once a friend or mentor. Maybe they embody the path the hero could have taken. When the final showdown happens, the opponent's presence should shake something loose inside the hero. Their words, their moves, their style—it should all say something about who they are and why the hero must defeat them to move forward.

Designing the fight itself is where you get to have a bit of fun, but even this part is best when guided by theme. Let's say your hero has struggled with controlling their rage. Earlier in the story, they might've fought wildly, recklessly, even winning with brute force. But now, in the final showdown, they win through clarity, discipline, and timing. Every movement shows who they've become. Maybe they finally use a technique their master taught them—but in their own way. Maybe they counter a move that defeated them earlier in the story. These callbacks tie everything together and make the climax satisfying.

This is also the moment for emotional release. Let your character struggle, hesitate, falter—then push through. The best fights feel like they could go either way. The hero earns the win not because they're suddenly unbeatable, but because they've changed. They've become the person who *can* win. If you're working with ChatGPT, this is where the tool shines. Just describe the emotional goal of the scene—"I want my hero to defeat their former best friend without killing them, proving they've found peace"—and ChatGPT can help you brainstorm moves, dialogue, and emotional beats that hit those notes.

Dialogue is optional in a final showdown, but when used well, it can be devastating. A line spoken in an earlier scene can return here with new meaning. A promise made can be fulfilled. Or broken. Sometimes, a single word can cut deeper than any blade. Let your characters speak—briefly and meaningfully—if it serves the moment. Or let the silence say it all. In martial arts stories, what's unspoken often hits hardest.

The pacing of your final fight matters too. It doesn't have to be long. Some of the most memorable confrontations are short but intense. Others are drawn out like duels of endurance. The key is escalation. Start with cautious probing. Let the characters test each other. Then turn it up. Break the rhythm. Make the hero struggle. Let the tide shift. And finally, let the last few exchanges say it all—through action, through decision, through the one move that ends it.

And don't forget the emotional aftermath. Once the fight is over, what's left? Broken bones? Reconciliation? Loss? Peace? Closure? This is the echo of the showdown. It lingers in the silence that follows. In that moment, your hero isn't just victorious—they're *complete*. Or at least changed. When you write your martial arts story with the final showdown in place from the start, everything else—training scenes, setbacks, rivalries, inner battles—builds toward that emotional release.

So take the time to write the ending first. Picture it clearly. Where are they standing? What do they see, feel, fear? What's the first move? What's the last move? What are the consequences? Then ask ChatGPT to help fill in the gaps. It can build you a structure that serves this ending. It can help you design the rival. It can show you how to weave the right beats into earlier parts of the story. When you start with the ending, you're not guessing anymore—you're aiming. And that aim gives every part of your story power.

Because in martial arts fiction, the ultimate showdown isn't just the climax—it's the soul. And when you build your story around that soul from the very beginning, you're writing something unforgettable. Something that fights, speaks, and breathes all at once.

Letting ChatGPT Build Your Plot, Blow by Blow

When you're trying to write a martial arts story in a single day, you don't have time to second-guess every turn in your plot. You need momentum. You need clarity. And you need a system that keeps feeding you ideas without burning you out. That's exactly where ChatGPT becomes your creative sparring partner—quick, sharp, and always ready with the next move. Whether you're building a tournament-style story with multiple fight scenes or a quiet tale of inner discipline and redemption, ChatGPT can help you construct your plot *blow by blow*, making sure every step of your story leads cleanly to the next.

The first thing to understand is that ChatGPT doesn't need to be fed a perfect pitch. You can come in rough. In fact, the vaguer the initial prompt, the more variety you might get. Try starting with something like: "Give me a basic martial arts story idea with a rival and a tournament setting," or "What's a strong plot for a martial arts story about an ex-fighter pulled back into the ring?" Right away, you'll be given a clean and usable plot—usually with a beginning, middle, and end, plus emotional stakes.

But once you've got that framework, you don't want to stop there. You want to go deeper. You want to get specific. That's when you start asking for the blow-by-blow. Not just in terms of fight choreography, but in story structure. For example, you can say, "Break this plot into ten beats that each contain a turning point or emotional shift." ChatGPT will give you a scene-by-scene roadmap. Now you know what happens after the first fight, when the rival appears again, when the protagonist experiences doubt, when the master reveals a painful truth, and how the buildup leads to the final showdown.

This kind of plotting is perfect for martial arts fiction, which lives on escalation. Your fights should build in intensity, but so should the emotional and thematic stakes. The first fight might be a wake-up call. The second a moment of humiliation. The third a moral crossroads. The final fight is never just a fight—it's the result of all that came before it. When ChatGPT helps you map that out, it's easier to keep the emotional continuity intact, even when you're writing at high speed.

If your story involves multiple matches—like a bracket tournament, street fights across a city, or a series of lessons—ask ChatGPT to structure those as "progressive fight encounters." You can say, "Design four fight scenes that increase in difficulty and emotional weight for my hero, ending in a final confrontation with their former master." You'll get a progression that gives you space to explore different opponents, fighting styles, and emotional beats, all while marching toward the climax with precision.

And then there's character-driven plotting. You can use ChatGPT to let your characters shape the direction of the story by giving it prompts like, "Based on this character's fear of failure and their mentor's tough love approach, what kind of conflict should emerge halfway through the story?" Or, "My hero is too reliant on brute strength—how should this flaw be exposed in a major fight scene?" These moments aren't just filler—they're plot-defining. You're letting character psychology push the action, just like in a great martial arts film where every punch is personal.

You can even ask for scene descriptions. Don't just say "help me with the plot." Say, "Give me a gritty, high-stakes alley fight where my hero has to win but refuses to fight dirty like his opponent." Or, "What happens when the hero refuses to finish the match, choosing mercy over victory, and the crowd turns on them?" These kinds of prompts will give you cinematic detail and emotional layers, and they'll make your writing flow faster because the hard creative work is already halfway done for you.

Let's say you've got your structure: Act One introduces the flawed hero. Act Two brings training, trials, and rivalries. Act Three culminates in the final showdown. Now you can go scene by scene with ChatGPT. "What should happen in the first ten pages of a martial arts script where the hero is a disgraced fighter working in a bar?" You'll get dialogue ideas, setting details, maybe even a plot twist you didn't expect. Then follow it up with, "What's the best way to introduce the mentor figure in this story?" Or, "How should I write a training montage in novel format?"

Even better, you can use ChatGPT to play "what if" with your plot. What if the rival and the hero have the same master? What if the final match is rigged? What if the protagonist breaks their code in a moment of rage and loses everything? Just ask: "What if the hero breaks their master's rule and it costs them their only chance at redemption?" Now you're not just getting a story—you're getting drama, character growth, and stakes that matter.

The more you engage with ChatGPT, the better your story gets. You're not guessing what comes next—you're responding to suggestions, reshaping them, sharpening them. It's like shadowboxing with a perfect partner—never tired, always ready. And when you get stuck, which happens to every writer, you can prompt your way out: "My plot feels flat after the second fight—how can I shake things up?" Or, "What would be an unexpected twist that still fits with my story's emotional arc?"

What's powerful about this method is that it gives you confidence. You don't have to sit staring at the screen, hoping for inspiration. You just ask a smart question, get a clean response, and keep moving. You can write the entire plot in an hour, then start fleshing out scenes with character dialogue, description, and action choreography, all with ChatGPT feeding your creativity.

So don't treat plotting like a solo act. Let ChatGPT get in the ring with you. Ask for guidance. Test your scenes. Adjust your pacing. Get the big story arcs and the small emotional beats. And if you're writing the whole thing in one day, this kind of collaboration is your secret weapon. By the time you reach the final blow, you won't just have a plot. You'll have a fully-formed story that hits hard and never lets up.

Understanding What Makes a Martial Arts Story Work

There's a certain pulse that runs through every martial arts story that really works. You feel it right away—it's not just the kicks, punches, or pressure point takedowns. It's not even the high-flying choreography or the tournament arcs. What makes a martial arts story stick is what's *underneath* all that. It's the soul of the story. The discipline. The struggle. The code. If you strip away the visual spectacle, what you're left with is a story about transformation, identity, and the collision between belief systems. And that's what makes a martial arts narrative not only entertaining, but emotionally gripping.

A good martial arts story works because it's always about more than the fight. The fight is just the lens. Through it, we see who the character is and what they're made of. Whether it's a street-level story about survival, or a stylized epic full of ancient scrolls and secret techniques, what grounds it all is *character*. The fighter must want something—and not just a trophy. They might want redemption, revenge, purpose, clarity, or simply to belong. And the fighting style they use becomes a direct extension of that desire. So if your story is going to work, it has to start with that core emotional engine.

Another thing that separates the great from the forgettable is the *why* behind the violence. Martial arts stories are never about violence for its own sake. The most iconic tales show restraint. There's a tension between power and responsibility. Whether your hero avoids fighting until forced or trains obsessively for a righteous cause, the moment they step into conflict has to matter. Every blow has to carry weight—not just physically, but morally. The stakes need to feel personal. That's what elevates the showdown from spectacle to catharsis.

Philosophy plays a huge role here too. You don't need a full-on manifesto, but your story should have a set of beliefs that the characters either live by or struggle against. One character may believe that strength equals control. Another might be taught that true strength lies in compassion. These aren't just differences of opinion—they're the fuel for conflict. When your hero and antagonist represent opposing ideals, their eventual fight becomes a clash of worldviews. That's what makes it memorable. And that's why martial arts stories, even when simple on the surface, can go toe-to-toe with Shakespeare when it comes to drama.

Setting is another layer that makes these stories work. Martial arts fiction can take place anywhere: modern cities, feudal kingdoms, near-future dystopias, or hidden monasteries in the mountains. But no matter where it's set, the environment should reflect something about the story. A gritty urban setting might echo the hero's internal chaos. A quiet, snow-covered village might symbolize peace—or isolation. The setting isn't just a backdrop. It's a training ground, a battleground, a proving ground. It should enhance the tone and mirror the inner journey of your characters.

Let's talk about the mentor-student dynamic, a foundational element in martial arts fiction. This relationship is often where the heart of the story lives. The mentor isn't just there to teach technique—they're there to challenge, provoke, inspire, and sometimes frustrate the hero into growing. And when that relationship breaks or deepens, the story shifts. Whether your master is strict and stoic, quirky and cryptic, or mysterious and broken, they should represent a worldview your hero must eventually make their own—or break away from. Many martial arts stories work because the student isn't just trying to defeat an enemy—they're trying to live up to the ideals of the person who taught them.

The rival dynamic is just as important. Often, the rival reflects what the hero *could* become if they took a different path. Maybe the rival trains harder, or has a personal grudge, or shares the same goal but with darker motives. Great martial arts stories work when the rival isn't just an obstacle—but a mirror. Watching the hero and rival clash over and over gives the story tension, but also depth. You're watching two philosophies evolve in tandem, culminating in a final fight that isn't just about who's better—but who's *right*.

Another key element is how training is portrayed. In many other genres, training can feel like filler. But in martial arts fiction, it's essential. That's because training scenes aren't just about learning new techniques—they're about learning *the self*. A training montage that shows the hero sweating, falling, and failing isn't just there to show time passing. It's there to reflect struggle, dedication, growth. And each technique learned in training should pay off later—not just in terms of plot, but in terms of character evolution. Maybe they finally land a technique only when they overcome an emotional block. That's storytelling that hits with impact.

And then there's pacing. Martial arts stories work best when they balance stillness and movement. Not every scene should be a brawl. Moments of reflection, dialogue, and emotional tension make the action pop even more when it does arrive. The calm before the storm. The meditation before the match. A conversation with a mentor before a rival enters the dojo. These quieter moments make the louder ones more powerful. It's the rhythm of the story that gives it life, and martial arts narratives have one of the most distinct rhythms of any genre.

One more thing—when martial arts stories work, they *respect* the art. That doesn't mean you have to be a black belt to write a great fight scene. It means that the martial arts are never treated like a gimmick. They are presented with reverence, or at least with understanding. The way a fighter moves, the way they think, the way they approach a challenge—it all has to feel rooted in something real. Even if you're inventing your own fighting style or setting the story on Mars, the martial discipline has to feel earned, lived in, internalized. That's what makes the fights matter. That's what makes the audience believe.

And remember, with ChatGPT, you can test all of this quickly. Want to create a compelling mentor-student relationship? Ask for a sample scene. Need a rival with a deep emotional backstory? Generate one instantly. Stuck on the emotional subtext of a fight? Let ChatGPT describe it for you. The more you dig into what makes martial arts stories tick, the more tools you'll have ready when writing yours in a day.

In the end, what makes a martial arts story work is the same thing that makes a warrior worth rooting for. Integrity. Passion. Struggle. A willingness to face the hardest parts of themselves. When you write with that in mind—focusing on character, conflict, philosophy, and transformation—you're not just writing a fight story. You're writing something that hits, that lingers, and that leaves a mark long after the final blow is delivered.

Choosing the Right Martial Arts Style for the Story

One of the most exciting parts of writing a martial arts story is choosing the fighting style your characters will use. But this isn't just about picking what looks cool in a fight scene. The martial art itself should say something about the character and the story you're trying to tell. Different disciplines have different histories, philosophies, techniques, and tones. Choosing the right one can elevate your story from good to unforgettable. It shapes how your characters move, how they think, what values they hold, and even what kinds of enemies challenge them most.

The first question to ask yourself is: what kind of story are you telling? A grounded, street-level revenge tale might feel very different from a mythic wuxia fantasy, and each would benefit from a different fighting style. Boxing or Muay Thai suits a gritty urban setting where power, resilience, and impact are everything. Tai Chi or Aikido might be better suited to a philosophical, introspective story where balance and control are the focus. If your story is fast-paced and flashy, something like Capoeira or Wushu might match the rhythm. And if you're working in a setting that's historical or fantastical, you might invent your own martial art—something that reflects the culture or world you're building.

What a fighting style represents is just as important as what it looks like. Karate is often about discipline and tradition. Brazilian Jiu-Jitsu focuses on leverage and patience, often used to show how the smaller, weaker fighter can overcome a stronger opponent. Wing Chun is close-range and economical—great for a character who keeps things tight and controlled. Krav Maga is brutal and efficient, often taught to soldiers and used in life-or-death situations, so it fits characters who are all about survival and damage. Each art carries a story with it. And that story can feed directly into the emotional arc of your character.

Let's say your hero is hot-headed and impulsive. Maybe they start off using a more aggressive or unrefined style like street brawling or kickboxing, but as they grow emotionally, they're introduced to a more measured discipline like traditional Kung Fu. The evolution in style mirrors their personal growth. Or imagine a character who refuses to fight at all but is eventually forced to learn self-defense. Aikido, which is all about redirecting an attacker's energy without hurting them, might be the perfect fit. These aren't just aesthetic choices—they're symbolic ones.

If you're writing a tournament-based story, you can use multiple styles to create contrast and tension. A Muay Thai fighter might clash with a Taekwondo practitioner in a stylistic chess match of power versus speed. A grappler versus a striker. A disciplined student versus a wild card with unpredictable moves. Each fight becomes not just a battle of skill but a commentary on the values those styles represent. This approach makes your fight scenes feel like conversations—each style saying something about the person using it.

You also want to think about the world your story takes place in. If you're working in a realistic modern setting, using real-world martial arts might anchor your story in authenticity. Readers will recognize Judo, Karate, or MMA, and if you treat those styles with respect, it adds credibility. But if your story takes place in a fantasy realm or post-apocalyptic wasteland, you have the freedom to create hybrid or original styles that blend swordplay, elemental control, acrobatics, or psychic energy. You can build entire cultures around how a fictional martial art is practiced and passed down, turning it into a storytelling device in its own right.

ChatGPT can help you figure this out quickly. You can ask something like, "What martial arts style fits a character who is calm and analytical, but deeply repressed emotionally?" or "Give me three martial arts styles for a story about a dystopian underground fighting league." You'll get options that suit your character's psychology and your story's atmosphere. You can even explore combinations—what if your hero blends Judo with parkour, or Kung Fu with dance?

Ask ChatGPT to brainstorm fusion styles, and you'll have something original that still feels grounded in martial tradition.

If you want to create your own martial art entirely, start with the philosophy. What does the style believe in? Is it about preservation or destruction? Balance or dominance? Honor or deception? From there, decide what kind of movements it uses—long-range strikes, grappling, counters, weapons, or even pressure point attacks. Then build a name, a history, a set of rituals. With ChatGPT, you can build a full martial system in minutes. Just give a short description—"Design a martial art created by desert nomads who fight with cloth wraps and wind techniques"—and watch the story unfold.

Don't forget that the martial art can also be a source of conflict. Maybe your character was raised in a school that banned certain techniques, but now they must use them to survive. Maybe their fighting style is outdated and mocked, and they must prove it still has value. Maybe they left their dojo after breaking its code, and now they fight in secret using forbidden moves. These choices drive narrative tension and deepen the personal stakes of every punch and kick.

Martial arts aren't just moves—they're belief systems made physical. They're histories written in sweat and repetition. They carry honor, trauma, tradition, rebellion, and sometimes contradiction. Choosing the right one makes your story feel lived-in, real, and connected to something bigger than just action. And when your characters fight, the audience isn't just watching technique—they're watching meaning unfold in motion.

So take a little time to consider what style suits your story. Whether it's real or imagined, flashy or humble, brutal or graceful, the martial art your character practices should feel like a perfect fit for who they are—and who they're becoming. Use ChatGPT to test ideas fast, generate details, and shape the style into something that fits your world. Because in the end, the right martial art doesn't just define your hero's fighting stance—it defines their soul.

Fictional or Real: Building Martial Arts Worlds

Martial arts stories can take place anywhere—from the quiet stillness of a temple courtyard to the electric roar of an underground arena. But one of the biggest creative decisions you'll make as a writer is whether to base your world in reality or let your imagination run wild. Do you anchor your story in the real-world traditions of Okinawan Karate, Shaolin Kung Fu, or Brazilian Jiu-Jitsu? Or do you build your own martial arts universe from scratch, complete with made-up disciplines, rival schools, mystical philosophies, and fighting tournaments in volcano-crater arenas? The choice you make here changes everything—your tone, your rules, your themes, and your characters.

There's no right answer. Both approaches can be powerful. What matters is that you commit to your world and build it with consistency. A martial arts world, real or fictional, has to feel like it *functions*. There should be codes of honor, systems of training, rivalries between styles or schools, and a reason why people fight in the first place. Whether you're dealing with traditional dojos in Tokyo or sand-blasted fight pits in a dystopian future, the culture of combat needs to feel lived-in, logical, and meaningful.

Let's start with real-world settings. If you're writing a story grounded in modern or historical reality, you've got a rich tapestry to draw from. You can explore martial arts in specific cultural contexts—like Muay Thai in Thailand, Judo in Japan, or Capoeira in Brazil. Each of these arts carries its own history, philosophy, and community. Using real martial arts adds instant credibility to your story. You can explore questions of lineage, tradition, and authenticity. A character might be trying to live up to their family dojo's legacy or fighting to modernize a fading discipline. These kinds of conflicts are very real in martial arts circles, and when portrayed well, they give your story weight and authenticity.

But writing real-world martial arts also comes with responsibility. You have to respect the culture and practice you're portraying. That doesn't mean you have to become a black belt overnight—but it does mean doing some research. What are the core values of this art? What's its history? What kind of training do students go through? Even just reading a few first-hand accounts or watching documentary footage can make your scenes feel richer. And if you're short on time, you can lean on ChatGPT to summarize the key philosophies and practices of real-world styles to incorporate into your story without misrepresenting them.

Now let's step into the realm of the fictional. Creating your own martial arts world gives you freedom—freedom to design your own fighting styles, your own rules of honor, your own training rituals, even your own physics if you want to mix in fantasy or sci-fi. Maybe you're building a world where martial arts are used to control elemental forces. Maybe there are ancient scrolls that contain lost techniques. Maybe every city has its own dojo representing a different animal style, and there's an inter-dojo war brewing. You can be as grounded or as mystical as you like—as long as your rules stay consistent.

The best fictional martial arts stories still feel real because they echo truth. Even if your characters are flipping through the air or sending shockwaves through the ground, the emotions, motivations, and discipline have to be relatable. Audiences are willing to suspend disbelief if they feel the heart of the story is grounded. So even in a world where fighting spirits can be summoned from tattoos, there's still a student struggling with self-doubt, a rival seeking vengeance, a master hiding a painful past. That's what makes it all work.

With ChatGPT, building fictional martial arts worlds becomes a blast. You can prompt it with something like, "Create a fictional martial arts system based on manipulating soundwaves through movement," and it'll help you invent techniques, stances, ranks, and rituals. You can take that even further by asking, "What kind of culture would emerge around a martial art that can only be taught through dreams?" Suddenly, you're not just making a style—you're building a mythology.

Fictional martial arts also give you freedom with your setting. Want to write a story where fighters duel on floating islands and use energy drawn from ancient crystals? Go for it. Want to set your story in a cyberpunk city where martial arts are used to hack bio-enhanced enemies? Do it. The trick is to tie your setting and your martial art style together. The world should feel like it grew around the way people fight. A world where martial arts are sacred will feel different from one where they're outlawed or commercialized.

You can also blend the real and the fictional. Many great martial arts stories do exactly that. Maybe your hero starts with traditional Judo, but later learns a forbidden style that taps into supernatural abilities. Maybe your setting is modern day, but there's a hidden underworld where ancient fighting traditions are kept secret. These hybrids give you the best of both worlds—the realism of grounded discipline and the creativity of imaginative flair.

Another cool way to use world-building is through hierarchy and systems. Maybe fighters are ranked not by belts but by tattoos, scars, or unique weapons. Maybe there's a council of masters who determine the rules of combat, or maybe there's no order at all—just chaos and survival. Create factions, rival schools, ancient grudges. Build history into your setting, even if it's just hinted at. A single line like "That move's been banned since the Fire Scroll Massacre" can imply a whole backstory that sparks curiosity and immersion.

Don't forget to think about how people in your world view martial arts. Are fighters respected like monks? Treated like celebrities? Hunted like criminals? Is martial arts something taught openly, or something you have to risk everything to learn? How the world responds to martial arts tells us a lot about the story's moral compass. Use it to deepen your themes.

So, whether you're crafting a modern dojo drama or an epic fantasy of fist and fury, your world needs structure, values, and consequences. It should feel like a place where martial arts mean something—more than spectacle, more than strength. They should represent survival, tradition, rebellion, identity, or even transcendence.

Use ChatGPT to brainstorm your setting, your systems, your fighting styles, your world history. Build it one punch at a time. Ask for "five fictional martial arts tournaments and what makes each one unique," or "describe a culture where martial arts are a form of poetry." The more specific you get, the more vivid your world becomes.

In the end, real or imagined, your martial arts world needs to feel alive. It has to breathe. And whether it's rooted in the real or soaring into the fantastical, what matters most is that your readers believe in it—because your characters believe in it. And when they fight, we feel it. Not just the strikes, but the story behind every one of them.

Bringing the Training Montage to Life on the Page

There's no more iconic moment in a martial arts story than the training montage. We've seen it a thousand times on screen—jump cuts of sweat, screams, bruises, and breakthroughs. From Rocky pounding meat in a freezer to Daniel LaRusso balancing on one leg at sunset, these sequences are burned into the collective storytelling brain. But when it comes to writing a martial arts story on the page, the montage doesn't come with an editing timeline or a soundtrack. You've got to create the same feeling with nothing but words. And if you do it right, your reader will hear the music in their head anyway.

The training sequence isn't just a time skip—it's an emotional arc compressed into movement. It's where your character begins to change. Their body grows stronger, yes, but so does their will. Their worldview is challenged, their weaknesses are exposed, and their habits are broken down and rebuilt. So when writing your training montage, your goal isn't just to show exercises. Your goal is to dramatize transformation. And that means every punch, every failure, every ache should carry emotional weight.

Start with where your character is at the beginning of the training. Are they arrogant? Defeated? Undisciplined? You want your montage to reflect where they *start*, so the progress feels meaningful. A training scene that begins with the protagonist collapsing halfway through a kata or losing their temper during sparring sets the tone. Show the tension. Show the resistance. This is not just a workout—it's a war with the self.

Next, vary the challenges. You can use physical training—endurance runs, weapons drills, balance exercises—but pair it with internal struggle. The best montages show us that training is *mental*. Let the master speak in cryptic lessons that the student initially mocks or misunderstands. Let the hero fail a seemingly simple task over and over. Have them question why they're doing this. That moment where they finally "get it" will hit so much harder if we've seen the frustration build.

Sensory detail matters here. Instead of listing actions like "he punched the bag" or "she climbed the mountain," give us texture. Let us feel the sting in the knuckles. Let us smell the dust kicked up from the mat. Let us hear the sharp snap of the bamboo staff each time it cracks against the air—or their back. The more visceral your writing, the more cinematic the moment becomes in the reader's mind.

Pacing is important too. You want the montage to feel like it moves forward with rhythm. Use shorter sentences to create a sense of urgency, intensity, and repetition. Then slow it down for moments of reflection. Maybe your hero catches their reflection in a puddle or a mirror and sees something different for the first time. Maybe they're finally able to do a move they've failed a dozen times before—and don't even realize it until the master nods in approval for the first time.

This is also a perfect place for symbolic or thematic imagery. Maybe your character climbs a steep hill every morning while carrying a heavy bag, symbolizing the emotional burden they're working through. Maybe they try to light a candle in a rainstorm using only a single match—and fail day after day until they learn how to shield the flame with their body. These moments are memorable because they're visual metaphors for the character's journey. Ask ChatGPT to help you come up with "unusual martial arts training exercises that symbolize inner growth," and you'll have a page full of striking, original ideas that write themselves into unforgettable scenes.

Your master figure can be a strong emotional thread throughout. Whether they're harsh, humorous, silent, or mystical, their presence is the spine of the training arc. And how your character responds to them—whether with resistance, admiration, rebellion, or longing—deepens the relationship. The training montage is often where that bond is forged, tested, or broken. Maybe your character wants the master's approval and never gets it. Maybe the master refuses to teach them the final move unless they prove themselves worthy through something other than fighting. This dynamic adds tension and heart to your training scenes.

And don't be afraid to insert small moments of silence. Let the training breathe. A quiet sunrise. A cold bowl of rice. A bandaged hand trembling just before wrapping around the training weapon again. These in-between beats give the montage gravity. They tell us that this process is changing the person, not just their body.

You also have the option of breaking up the training montage across your story. You don't have to cram it all into one chapter. Let it appear in flashes. A day of failure here. A surprising breakthrough there. A new technique learned right when it's needed most. This approach feels more natural and allows for the kind of long-form development that mirrors real training—slow, painful, but rewarding.

When you're writing quickly—especially in a one-day sprint—ChatGPT is a game-changer here. You can say, "Describe a martial arts training montage where the student goes from reckless to controlled," or "Give me sensory details for a fight-based endurance drill in a forest setting." You'll get powerful language, imagery, and progression you can either use as-is or modify to match your character and tone. The more specific your prompt, the richer the response. You can build a whole training arc in an hour and have it feel like it took weeks of sweat and pain.

The key is to treat the montage not like a shortcut, but like a pivotal part of the story. It's the turning point where the reader starts to believe that the final showdown might actually be possible. That's a big deal. That's why it deserves your best writing.

So when you sit down to bring your training montage to life, don't just focus on the muscles and movements. Focus on the mind. On the change. On the quiet in the noise, and the discipline in the chaos. Build the scene with rhythm, with pain, with heart. Because when your reader reaches that final fight and sees the result of all that effort—they'll feel every drop of sweat in the air.

Inventing a Villain worth Fighting

In martial arts stories, the final battle is only as powerful as the villain standing across from your hero. A well-crafted antagonist isn't just there to lose in the end—they embody the central conflict, both physically and emotionally. They challenge the hero on every level, not just in combat, but in belief. They're the mountain the hero has to climb, the mirror that reflects their darkest fear, and sometimes the ghost of who they could've become if they took a different path. If you want your martial arts story to hit hard and stick with readers, then you need to invent a villain truly worth fighting.

The first step in building your villain is figuring out what they *represent*. Great martial arts antagonists aren't just tough—they stand for something. Maybe they believe strength is the only truth in the world. Maybe they hide their own fear under layers of cruelty. Maybe they're a former student of the same master who took a darker path. The fight at the end of your story shouldn't just be about fists flying—it should be a clash of philosophies. When your hero punches them, it should feel like they're punching through doubt, fear, guilt, or a broken system.

This is why a villain in martial arts fiction needs depth. They might be ruthless or brutal, but they also need conviction. They must believe in their actions, even if those beliefs are twisted. The most chilling villains are often the ones who don't see themselves as evil—they think they're right. Maybe they believe the world is too weak and they're the necessary correction. Maybe they're protecting something in their own broken way. When you build your villain this way, their presence adds weight to every scene, even when they're not there.

You also want your villain to be *personal*. It's not enough for them to be the final boss in a tournament bracket. They should connect to the hero's emotional journey in some way. This could be literal—a former friend, a sibling, a master turned traitor—or symbolic, like someone who carries the opposite philosophy or reflects the hero's past mistakes. When the hero faces them, it shouldn't just be a contest of skill. It should hurt. It should mean something. The fight should settle more than the score.

The villain's fighting style also tells a story. Are they precise and emotionless, using sharp, controlled strikes that mirror their cold worldview? Or are they chaotic and overwhelming, reflecting an inner fury they can barely contain? If your hero fights with restraint and balance, the villain might fight with unrelenting aggression. If your hero is scrappy and instinctive, the villain might be a calculated technician. Contrast in fighting style emphasizes contrast in values. You can even use physical scars, injuries, or posture to suggest a lifetime of war—making the villain feel like they've *earned* their menace.

And don't be afraid to give your villain their own arc. Maybe they weren't always this way. Maybe they once believed in something noble, but betrayal or loss twisted their path. Giving them a tragic backstory doesn't mean you have to justify their actions, but it makes them believable. When you write the final confrontation, let the reader feel that this person was shaped by pain, just like the hero was. They just made different choices. That's what makes the final fight bittersweet and unforgettable.

ChatGPT can be a huge help in building these kinds of layered antagonists. You can start with a simple prompt like, "Create a martial arts villain who believes peace can only be earned through dominance," and expand from there. Ask follow-ups like, "What is this villain's fighting style?" or "Describe their relationship with the hero's master." Before you know it, you've got a full character with motivation, history, philosophy, and technique. Not just someone to lose—but someone who pushes your hero to their limit.

And let's talk about presence. A strong villain doesn't need to be in every scene, but their influence should be felt throughout. Maybe your hero hears about them before they meet. Maybe their legend grows—whispers in the dojo, tales from old fighters, brutal signs of their rise to power. When they finally appear, the reader should feel it. That first scene with the villain should send a chill down the spine, not because of what they say or do, but because of what they represent. This is the person who will test everything the hero stands for.

Your villain should also *challenge the reader*. Not in a way that makes us root for them, but in a way that makes us understand them. Their arguments should almost make sense. Their vision should be seductive. Maybe they promise order in a chaotic world, or strength in a world full of weakness. The reader should feel that if the hero wasn't careful, they could easily have ended up the same way. That moral tension is what elevates the final conflict—it becomes a fight for the hero's soul, not just survival.

If you want to take it further, give your villain a moment of quiet reflection. Let them speak about what they've lost, what they believe. Don't rush to villainize them with cheap evil. Make them human. Because when the final punch lands—when the hero stands victorious—it shouldn't feel like defeating a monster. It should feel like overcoming the worst version of the self.

You can also ask ChatGPT to roleplay your villain. Type, "Act as my martial arts story's villain and explain why you're not the bad guy," and see what comes back. You'll get voice, tone, and attitude you can pull directly into your dialogue and scenes. Do this a few times, and you'll know exactly how this character thinks and fights, and how they see your hero.

In the end, a great martial arts villain isn't just tough—they're tragic, compelling, believable, and utterly necessary. They exist to break the hero down so the hero can rise back up, stronger than before. They are the flame the protagonist must walk through to emerge fully formed.

So build them carefully. Give them a voice. Give them a history. Give them a reason. Because when the hero finally steps onto that stage, what makes the moment powerful isn't just who they're fighting—it's *why* they must win.

Turning Rivalries into Emotional Conflict

A rivalry in a martial arts story can be more than just an excuse to stage a cool fight. In fact, it *should* be more than that. When done right, a rivalry becomes one of the richest sources of emotional fuel in the entire narrative. It's not just a battle of skill—it's personal. It's complicated. It carries history, tension, longing, resentment, respect, and sometimes even love. A great rivalry doesn't just raise the stakes of a fight—it deepens the entire story. And in martial arts fiction, where personal transformation is everything, turning a rivalry into emotional conflict is what gives your story weight and resonance.

So where does a great rivalry begin? It starts with *shared history*. Rivals are rarely strangers. Maybe they trained together as kids. Maybe they were once close friends, or teammates, or students under the same master. Maybe one was always slightly better—or slightly worse—and that imbalance has never healed. The best rivalries are born from familiarity. They know each other's strengths, weaknesses, and secrets. And that familiarity makes every interaction charged. When they fight, they're not just trying to win—they're trying to prove something. To themselves. To each other. To the world.

Let's say your hero and their rival were once best friends. They trained together, sweated together, maybe even dreamed together. But something drove them apart. One wanted to follow the traditional path of discipline and control. The other craved power and recognition. That divergence, that split, becomes the emotional core of the rivalry. It's no longer just about who's stronger—it's about whose philosophy *matters*. When they meet in the final showdown, it's not just fists meeting fists. It's two ideologies colliding, two broken hearts trying to find closure in combat.

On the flip side, maybe your characters *never* liked each other. One was the dojo favorite, the golden child. The other, always overlooked, ignored, underestimated. That tension simmers over time until it explodes. This kind of rivalry is all about validation. One character is fighting to prove they belong. The other is fighting to stay on top. Again, the fight isn't just physical—it's emotional. Every block, strike, and counter is soaked in years of resentment.

With ChatGPT, you can easily build these dynamics. Just say, "Create a rivalry between two martial artists who trained under the same master but took opposing paths," and you'll get a full backstory in seconds. You can then dig deeper. Ask, "What kind of emotional conflict would arise if one of them blamed the other for the master's death?" Now you've got layers. Now you've got fire.

One of the most effective ways to deepen a rivalry is to give it *moments of tenderness*. A flash of empathy. A half-smile before the match. A shared memory. These moments confuse the hero. They blur the line between enemy and friend. And they remind the reader that this isn't a typical hero vs. villain setup—it's a relationship with scars. One powerful scene could be a quiet conversation before a fight. Maybe the rival admits they never hated the hero—they just couldn't forgive themselves. Or maybe they reveal they've been training all these years not to win, but to earn the hero's respect. That kind of emotional depth makes the fight unforgettable.

The rivalry should also shape your hero's growth. The rival is often the character who shows the hero what *not* to become—or what they *could* become, if they fail. Maybe the rival is consumed by vengeance, and the hero sees their own path reflected in that obsession. Maybe the rival used to believe in honor but gave it up for power, and the hero must reclaim that belief for both of them. These inner conflicts elevate the rivalry from competition to confrontation of the self.

The structure of the story can lean on the rivalry too. You don't have to wait until the end for them to fight. Let them clash early—maybe the rival wins. Let them cross paths again and again. Maybe they fight in a tournament, then have a quiet moment of reflection later. Maybe the rival saves the hero's life during a surprise attack. Each moment becomes a thread in the emotional knot that the final confrontation will untie—or tighten. ChatGPT can help you outline these beats quickly. Ask, "Give me five escalating scenes that show tension growing between my martial arts protagonist and their rival," and you'll get a dramatic arc ready to write.

Even the rival's fighting style should reflect their personality and their relationship with the hero. If the hero is calm and defensive, maybe the rival is aggressive and unpredictable. If the hero is technical and patient, maybe the rival is flashy and arrogant. These differences make their fights more than just exciting—they're visual metaphors. Every movement becomes character development.

And what if the rival wins? Or walks away? Or refuses to fight? These choices shake the foundation of the story and can say just as much as a knockout punch. Maybe the rival was never the real enemy. Maybe they just wanted to be seen. To be heard. To be remembered.

You can also give your rival their own journey. Let them question themselves. Let them evolve. Maybe they lose a match and it humbles them. Maybe they realize their hatred was misplaced. When both characters change across the story, their final meeting becomes even more powerful. They're not just opponents—they're reflections.

Martial arts is about balance. Rivalries are the perfect place to explore imbalance and restoration. Two people. One path. Two outcomes. When you tap into the emotional roots of a rivalry, the fights become intimate. The story becomes alive. And the readers stay hooked because it's no longer about who wins—it's about *why it matters*.

So lean into the conflict. Build the history. Explore the pain. And when your hero finally stands across from their rival, let every unspoken word, every missed opportunity, every moment of shared memory come flooding back. That's the fight your readers will remember. That's the kind of rivalry that makes a martial arts story hit straight to the heart.

Building Supporting Characters with Heart and Skill

While the hero might throw the final punch and stand in the spotlight at the end, a martial arts story is never carried by the protagonist alone. The characters in the background—training partners, rivals, mentors, friends, even comic relief sidekicks—bring soul to the journey. They make the world feel lived in, they raise the emotional stakes, and they help define who the hero is by contrast or support. Writing a martial arts story in a day doesn't mean you skip the side characters. In fact, giving them heart and skill is what can make your story memorable beyond the fights.

Let's start with purpose. Every supporting character should serve a function. They can represent an aspect of the theme, challenge or reinforce the hero's growth, or act as emotional anchors throughout the narrative. Maybe you've got the wise but broken master who pushes the hero harder than necessary because they once failed a student. Or the childhood friend who isn't a fighter but always shows up when it counts. Maybe there's the cocky teammate who doesn't take anything seriously—until the stakes get real. When you write these characters with care, they don't feel like placeholders. They feel like people we've known.

In martial arts stories, the *dojo family* is often central. The bond between students training together forms its own type of brotherhood or sisterhood, and that energy can be the emotional core of the second act. Training partners push each other to the brink, offer encouragement during failure, or fall into competition that becomes either friendship or rivalry. These relationships are ripe with drama. Maybe one student is jealous of the protagonist's rapid progress. Maybe another is hurt when the hero starts training privately with the master. These conflicts don't need to be loud—but they should feel real.

Think about personality through movement. Martial arts is physical storytelling, and your supporting characters can express who they are in how they fight or train. A flashy fighter might crave attention or hide insecurities behind big moves. A rigid, form-perfect student might be terrified of making a mistake. A fighter who laughs during combat could be masking trauma or using humor as a defense. When you match personality with fighting style, your characters come alive even without long speeches or exposition. If you need help matching personality to technique, ChatGPT can do that easily—just ask, "What martial art style fits a character who is shy, precise, and avoids confrontation?"

Your mentor character deserves a little extra attention. They often play the emotional spine of a martial arts story, passing down not just skills but philosophy. They're the character who challenges the hero's beliefs, forces them to confront weakness, and, in many cases, holds a secret or pain of their own. Don't let them become a stock figure. Maybe they've lost their edge. Maybe they were once just like the villain. Maybe they don't believe the hero is ready, and that doubt causes friction. When your mentor is complex, every piece of advice they give carries more weight.

And don't forget about the emotional support characters. They might not fight, but they can be just as vital. A sibling, a partner, a teacher from school—someone who sees the hero beyond the dojo walls. These characters remind the audience what the hero is fighting *for*, not just *against*. Maybe it's a younger brother watching the hero train and trying to mimic them. Maybe it's a love interest who worries the hero is changing too much. These characters ground the story in relationships and emotion. They're the people who cheer from the sidelines—or walk away when things get too dangerous.

Conflict among the supporting cast is crucial too. They shouldn't all get along. Maybe one character thinks the hero is taking shortcuts. Maybe someone else refuses to forgive the rival, even when the hero starts to see them differently. These moments don't need to dominate the plot, but they make the story feel textured. They raise questions and offer different viewpoints. And in the end, they make the final victory feel like a team effort—even if only one person is throwing the final punch.

Even your antagonist can have a supporting cast. A loyal lieutenant. A shadowy advisor. A student who's too scared to leave the villain's side. These characters can offer glimpses into the villain's world and humanize them—or make them even more terrifying. Maybe they question the villain's tactics. Maybe they show hesitation. Or maybe they're more ruthless than the villain themselves. These dynamics can add tension and unpredictability to the antagonist's story.

Using ChatGPT, you can quickly breathe life into supporting characters. Try prompts like, "Give me three supporting characters for a martial arts story with distinct personalities and fighting styles," or "Describe a comic relief character who eventually proves themselves in a serious moment." The responses you get can shape dialogue, fighting techniques, backstories, and emotional beats—all tailored to your main plot.

And when in doubt, connect each character back to the *theme*. If your story is about inner peace versus rage, then let each character reflect a different way of dealing with anger. One bottles it up. One lets it explode. One turns it inward. Your hero's journey will be stronger when those around them are on similar, parallel, or opposing paths. That contrast fuels emotional arcs, not just action sequences.

At the end of the day, it's the supporting cast that fills the world out. They teach the hero lessons they didn't expect. They make the hero laugh when things get too serious. They break the hero's heart when they fail. And when the hero rises, it's because these characters helped them get there—through loyalty, challenge, or love.

So don't just throw in names to fill scenes. Give your supporting characters heart. Give them skill. Let them matter. Because in a martial arts story, every character is a fighter in their own way—even the ones who never throw a punch.

Using the Dojo as a Character

In martial arts stories, the dojo isn't just a setting—it's a living, breathing part of the narrative. Whether it's a humble back-alley training space, a sprawling temple carved into a mountaintop, or a concrete underground bunker buzzing with fluorescent lights and tension, the dojo can—and should—feel like a character in its own right. It holds memory. It imposes discipline. It shelters and tests everyone who steps inside. It evolves with the story. And if you write it well, readers or viewers will feel its presence just as strongly as they feel the protagonist's.

So what does it mean to treat the dojo as a character? It starts with thinking about what the dojo *represents*. For many martial arts students, a dojo isn't just a gym. It's a sacred place. It's where they shed their ego, bleed on the mats, face their failures, and grow in silence. For the characters in your story, the dojo should mean something personal. Maybe it's the last place the hero felt safe. Maybe it's where the villain once trained. Maybe it's neutral ground in a world full of chaos. What the dojo *means* will affect how your characters act within it.

The dojo often has a *personality* that matches the style and philosophy of the martial arts practiced there. A traditional Japanese dojo might be austere, quiet, filled with tatami mats, calligraphy scrolls, and a faint smell of incense. It demands respect. A gritty urban gym might be loud, crowded, and plastered with posters of past champions and brutal matches. It pulses with energy and ego. A remote forest dojo made from wood and stone might evoke a sense of retreat, reflection, and isolation. When describing the dojo in your writing, let those details drip with character. What's on the walls? How do the students behave when they walk in? Does the space feel warm or cold? Welcome or intimidating?

The *history* of the dojo is another powerful storytelling element. Maybe it was founded by a legendary master whose teachings have been twisted over time. Maybe it was destroyed during a feud and later rebuilt. Maybe it's haunted by an unresolved tragedy—like a student who died in training or a betrayal that split the class. All of this shapes how the current students view the space. Maybe they whisper about the past between rounds. Maybe the hero doesn't even know the whole story at first, and learning the truth becomes part of their arc.

Think about *how characters change when they're inside the dojo*. It should feel like stepping into a different world. Maybe the hot-headed rival becomes quiet and respectful in front of the training altar. Maybe the hero is confident everywhere except on the mats. The dojo can act as a mirror—revealing inner truths, cracking open emotional walls. It can be a place of healing or punishment, mentorship or manipulation. It can also become a battlefield when the story needs it, with the sacred space defiled by a sudden act of violence or betrayal.

The *rules* of the dojo also matter. Does everyone bow before entering? Are shoes forbidden? Are matches held in silence, with only the sound of breathing and movement? Or is it a no-holds-barred place where the only rule is survival? Establishing rules gives the dojo structure, and when someone breaks one, it carries weight. Maybe your antagonist refuses to bow. Maybe your hero gets expelled for striking someone outside of sparring. These moments of tension often hinge on how the dojo is treated—and how it "responds" to that treatment.

The *role of the master* in the dojo can also define its character. If the master is wise, calm, and traditional, the dojo might feel peaceful and disciplined. If the master is harsh, egotistical, or wounded, the dojo might reflect that with fear, intensity, or silence. You can even have multiple dojos in your story, each representing different ideologies, with the students clashing in the ring and in the streets. A story that revolves around rival dojos becomes more than just good versus evil—it becomes a battle of philosophies with the dojos acting like opposing houses in a larger martial arts world.

You can also show the *passage of time* through the dojo. Maybe it starts off cold and empty when the hero first arrives, but as they grow and form bonds, it becomes warmer, fuller, louder with life. Maybe it's pristine at the beginning, but slowly becomes worn and broken as internal conflict tears the students apart. The state of the dojo can reflect the state of the story.

If you're writing a story in a single day and don't want to get lost in worldbuilding, ChatGPT can help flesh this out quickly. Just prompt: "Describe a traditional martial arts dojo that feels ancient and haunted," or "Give me a futuristic dojo where cyber-enhanced fighters train under neon lights and strict AI rules." You'll get atmosphere, design details, rituals, and tone—everything you need to make the setting feel alive.

Don't be afraid to let the dojo *change*. Maybe it gets closed down. Maybe it's taken over by a rival. Maybe your protagonist is the one who must reopen it and carry on a legacy. The dojo's fate can run parallel to the hero's. When they rise, so does the dojo. When they fall, the mats go silent. And when the final fight happens, returning to the dojo can feel like coming home—or coming full circle.

Ultimately, a martial arts story without a dojo can still work—but one with a dojo that *feels* like a character is next level. It adds depth, identity, and emotional gravity to the story. It gives your characters a place to reflect, train, break, heal, and face who they really are. And for your readers, it becomes a place they can imagine walking into—hearing the sound of practice swords clashing, breathing in the scent of wood and sweat, and sensing the weight of tradition all around them.

So don't just write a room. Write a dojo that breathes. One that challenges your hero, holds your history, and becomes the stage where everything is won, lost, and learned.

Going Beyond the Tournament Trope

The martial arts tournament has become a staple of the genre—a bracketed battle structure where fighters face off round after round until only one remains. It's clean. It's familiar. It gives your story a built-in structure and a natural arc of escalating intensity. But if you want your martial arts story to stand out, you don't have to abandon the tournament—you just have to go *beyond* it. There's nothing wrong with a classic setup, but leaning too heavily on the tournament trope without adding depth or subversion can leave your story feeling predictable. The real magic happens when you dig beneath the surface and use the tournament as a launchpad, not a crutch.

First, let's acknowledge why tournaments work. They give the hero clear goals, obstacles, and pacing. They set the stage for multiple fight scenes, introduce colorful opponents, and naturally build tension as the hero climbs the ranks. There's a thrill in watching someone fight their way to the top. But the danger is that it can become formulaic. You don't want your story to feel like a string of random matches leading to a final boss fight. So how do you elevate the trope?

One of the simplest ways is to treat the tournament as *more than just a competition*. What does it *mean* to the characters involved? Is it a chance to redeem a family legacy? To expose corruption within the system? To infiltrate an enemy organization? Maybe the tournament is the only way the hero can find a long-lost rival, or the only place they can fight without legal consequences. Adding a personal or political motivation turns the tournament into a crucible for something much bigger than winning a trophy.

You can also play with *structure*. Not every tournament has to be a clean bracket. What if it's an underground event where matches are rigged, and the hero has to figure out how to survive while navigating backroom deals and ambushes? What if it's a round-robin with shifting alliances, forcing characters to fight friends—or team up with enemies? Or maybe there's a tiered system, where the fights start bare-knuckled in street alleys and end in front of an elite council in a sacred arena. You don't have to play by the rules, even if your characters do.

Another powerful move is to make the *emotional stakes* more important than the physical ones. Maybe the hero has to fight someone they care about—a sibling, a mentor, a student. Maybe they're facing someone who reminds them of who they used to be. Maybe the hero loses early on and has to decide whether to walk away or fight for something greater. In these moments, the tournament becomes a metaphor. It's not just about fighting other people—it's about fighting through grief, guilt, or fear.

You can also *shift the spotlight*. Most tournament stories center around the hero's journey to the top. But what if the focus is on a secondary character—someone we expect to fail, who surprises everyone? What if your protagonist isn't even in the tournament, but has to train someone who is? What if the villain is manipulating the entire event from behind the scenes? Changing the perspective opens up new narrative possibilities that still honor the energy of the trope without getting stuck in its repetition.

Sometimes, it's the *world outside* the tournament that brings your story to life. Maybe the event draws fighters from warring regions, and the tension bleeds out of the ring. Maybe spectators bet everything they own, and the fights spark class warfare. Maybe losing doesn't mean defeat—it means exile or death. When the stakes affect more than just the fighters, the tournament becomes a vehicle for larger societal conflict, and your story gains scale and urgency.

You can also infuse mystery into the format. What if no one knows who's hosting the tournament, or why? What if the real prize isn't gold or a title—but access to forbidden knowledge, a secret technique, or a hidden truth about the protagonist's past? Now your story has suspense and intrigue woven into the action, and every round becomes a step toward discovery.

And of course, ChatGPT can help you brainstorm these twists quickly. Try prompts like, "Give me five unique twists on the martial arts tournament structure," or "Create a tournament system where fighters must solve emotional conflicts as part of their advancement." You'll get fresh angles that help you break out of the typical mold without losing the core appeal of the format.

You don't have to abandon the classic scenes either. You can still have the intense stare-downs before a match, the montage of rising through the ranks, the surprise reversal in the finals. These are fun, familiar beats. But layer them with meaning. Let each opponent the hero faces symbolize a different struggle. One might fight with anger the hero once felt. Another might fight dirty, testing the hero's commitment to honor. By the time the final match arrives, it should feel like everything the hero has endured—physically, emotionally, spiritually—has led to that moment.

And maybe—just maybe—the most powerful choice is not to win. Maybe the hero forfeits, walks away, saves someone instead of finishing a fight. That kind of ending can subvert expectations while still delivering emotional truth. Victory doesn't always come from a knockout. Sometimes, it comes from restraint, growth, or sacrifice.

So go ahead—use the tournament. But don't stop there. Build meaning into every match. Twist the structure. Raise the stakes beyond the ring. And when the final bell rings, make sure it echoes with more than applause. Let it carry the weight of a story that dared to fight for more.

Honor, Discipline, and the Inner Journey

At the heart of every great martial arts story lies a journey that doesn't begin or end with fists—it begins within. The path of the warrior is not just paved with punches, blocks, and broken bones. It's shaped by honor, forged through discipline, and defined by transformation. While the physical battles may dazzle and thrill, it's the *inner journey*—the slow, painful evolution of the self—that gives a martial arts narrative its soul. And if you're writing a story that aims to resonate beyond the ring or the dojo, then this inner path is the one your hero must truly walk.

Let's start with honor. It's a concept woven into the fabric of nearly every martial arts tradition, but it means different things to different people. For some, honor is loyalty to their master. For others, it's about fighting only when necessary—or never striking first. Sometimes it's the promise to uphold a family legacy, or a vow never to kill. But whatever form it takes, honor in a martial arts story should *cost* something. If honor is easy, it doesn't mean anything. Let your protagonist be tested. Let them face choices that challenge their values. Maybe the only way to win a fight is to break a sacred rule. Maybe they watch someone dishonorable rise faster, and they're tempted to do the same. These are the crossroads where the inner journey becomes real.

Then there's discipline—the quiet, relentless backbone of the martial arts world. In story terms, discipline is often what separates a warrior from a brawler. It's what turns chaotic emotion into focused intention. The disciplined character is the one who trains when no one is watching, who gets up after failure, who doesn't need applause to keep going. But discipline isn't just physical. It's mental. Emotional. Spiritual. Your character's arc can—and should—include moments where their discipline falters. Maybe they lash out. Maybe they skip training. Maybe they turn their back on a master who pushes them too hard. These moments create depth, and they make the eventual return to discipline all the more powerful.

One of the most compelling elements of the inner journey is that it's usually invisible to others—but fully felt by the reader. On the surface, a character might just be learning a kata or preparing for a match. But inside, they're grappling with grief, shame, fear, or rage. They're trying to forgive someone. Or themselves. They're working through a loss, a betrayal, or a past mistake that still haunts them. That emotional training is just as grueling as any physical sparring session—and when done right, it makes every punch in your final fight land harder because we *know* what it took for the hero to get there.

In many martial arts stories, the hero starts off believing that strength means domination—winning fights, earning respect, being feared. But over time, they learn that true strength lies in restraint. In knowing when *not* to fight. In mastering one's ego. A beautifully written moment might be the hero standing still while others provoke them, choosing to breathe instead of lash out. Or walking away from a victory that comes at too high a cost. These moments are quiet, but they echo.

The inner journey can also be shaped by the master-student relationship. A good teacher doesn't just pass on techniques—they force the student to confront themselves. Maybe they speak in riddles that frustrate the hero. Maybe they push them past their breaking point, only to reveal that the real lesson was about patience or trust. Maybe the hero resents the master at first but later realizes that the harshness was a gift. This evolution often mirrors the hero's own relationship to discipline. First resistance. Then acceptance. Then mastery.

And let's not forget shame and failure—two of the most powerful forces on the path inward. Martial arts stories work so well because they're about people who fall. People who get knocked out in public, who disappoint their teachers, who get pushed to the edge of giving up. But then they rise. They rebuild. They face their own weakness and keep going anyway. That's the kind of storytelling that goes beyond spectacle and hits readers in the chest.

If you're short on time or feeling stuck, ChatGPT can help you uncover the layers of your character's inner arc. You can ask, "What kind of emotional journey might a martial artist go through if they broke their vow never to fight?" or "Describe a training scene where a fighter confronts their fear of failing their master." You'll get material that goes beyond surface action—moments that dig into the emotional foundation of your story.

Another way to weave honor and discipline into your story is through *contrast*. Maybe the rival character is talented but dishonorable—flashy, disrespectful, cruel. The contrast between them and the protagonist isn't just about fighting style—it's about values. That final clash becomes more than a match—it becomes a test of identity. Who will compromise? Who will stay true? That kind of thematic tension makes for unforgettable storytelling.

And finally, your hero's inner journey doesn't have to end with victory. Sometimes the real win is understanding. Peace. Clarity. Walking away with less applause but more truth. Maybe the protagonist doesn't take the top spot on the podium, but they make peace with their past. Maybe they pass on what they've learned to someone else. That ripple—of wisdom, of calm, of understanding—that's the real ending of a martial arts story. It's not just about how hard the hero hits. It's about how deep they've gone within themselves to find a new way to stand.

So as you craft your martial arts narrative, don't just think about the fights, the rivalries, the flashy techniques. Think about what's *inside* your hero. What are they fighting, not just outside, but within? What lesson will they learn about strength, control, and truth? Because in the end, that inner journey is what turns a fighter into a warrior—and a martial arts story into something that resonates long after the final bell.

How to Write a Martial Arts Story without Knowing Martial Arts

Here's the truth nobody tells you—*you don't have to be a black belt to write a powerful martial arts story*. You don't need to memorize the difference between a spinning back kick and a flying armbar. You don't need to have sparred in a ring or meditated in a mountain temple. What you *do* need is the ability to understand character, emotion, conflict, and growth—because that's what martial arts stories are really about. The fighting is just the expression. The story is always deeper. And if you can tap into that emotional truth, the rest will follow.

Let's clear something up right away: writing a martial arts story isn't about demonstrating your encyclopaedic knowledge of techniques. You're not writing a training manual. You're writing about people who *live* through martial arts. Their journey, their challenges, and their choices matter more than the specific name of a move. So instead of obsessing over whether your character uses Wing Chun or Kyokushin Karate, focus on *what fighting means to them*. Are they trying to prove something? Protect someone? Find peace? The emotional goal is the part that sticks with readers.

Now, that doesn't mean you should ignore authenticity. Readers can tell when a fight scene feels like it came from a cartoon, or when a dojo is described with the same detail as a generic gym. But you can build enough believability into your story without needing expert-level knowledge. Use ChatGPT to help you get the basics. Try prompting it with: "Explain the core philosophy of Taekwondo in two sentences," or "What kind of martial art focuses on throws and leverage?" You'll get quick, accurate context that you can work into your narrative naturally.

One of the best ways to fake it convincingly is to write from the *inside* out. Instead of describing the mechanics of every kick, write what the character *feels*. Their breath tightening. Their stance trembling. The sting in their knuckles. The rush of adrenaline. The self-doubt before a match. The silence in the dojo at night. These sensory details make the moment real, even if the reader doesn't know what a crescent kick is supposed to look like. They'll believe it because they'll feel it.

Another trick? Limit the technical detail to moments where it matters emotionally. You don't need to describe every step of a kata. But if your hero is trying to remember a move their master taught them—something that connects to their grief, or their growth—that's where a specific technique name lands with meaning. In that case, look up a few real moves, ask ChatGPT to explain one that fits your scene, and weave it in with emotional depth.

Character relationships are your secret weapon here. Use other characters—mentors, rivals, teammates—to talk about training, discipline, fear, or philosophy. A master's story about failing their own master. A rival mocking the hero's footwork. A teammate explaining how they overcame a fear of being hit. These conversations can carry the tone and insight of real martial arts wisdom, even if you're learning it as you go. You're not just building the world—you're giving the characters voices that reflect their connection to the art.

You also don't need to choreograph entire fight scenes move by move. That's a recipe for burnout. Instead, think in beats. A clash. A moment of hesitation. A dirty trick. A reversal. A moment of triumph. Ask ChatGPT: "Give me five beats for a martial arts fight between a calm, defensive fighter and an aggressive, reckless opponent." With that, you'll get a simple sequence that you can flesh out in your own words. You'll keep the flow of the story without getting lost in the weeds of whether the fighter turned their hip correctly during a roundhouse.

Also, remember that *why* your character fights is more interesting than *how*. Do they believe violence is a last resort? Are they trying to suppress rage? Are they addicted to the thrill of combat? These motivations shape the way they train, the way they approach opponents, and the kind of story you're telling. Once the inner conflict is clear, the fights become reflections of that inner struggle—and readers are far more likely to care about a sloppy brawler fighting for their sister than a perfect technician fighting for a trophy.

Let your research be functional, not overwhelming. You don't need to study 15 styles of martial arts to write one compelling story. You can look up a few core values—respect, humility, perseverance—and infuse those into your character's training and dialogue. A student bowing before stepping onto the mat, a fighter refusing to hit an opponent who's already down, a teacher scolding a student for fighting with anger instead of focus—these are the real ingredients of a martial arts story. And none of them require a black belt.

If you want to build authenticity into your setting, ChatGPT can generate dojos, rituals, traditions, training routines, and martial arts myths from around the world. Ask for five types of training exercises used in traditional Shaolin Kung Fu. Ask what a Muay Thai fighter might do to prepare mentally before a match. Ask what it means to become a sensei. Use these elements not to show off, but to deepen the world and ground the story in feeling and experience.

And if you want to invent your own martial art? Go for it. Just build it around a philosophy. Maybe your made-up style teaches that the first person to move has already lost. Maybe it relies on rhythm and timing, like dance. Maybe it's built around defending others rather than attacking. That idea will shape the techniques, rituals, and story moments, and ChatGPT can help you design the rest.

At the end of the day, writing a martial arts story without knowing martial arts is completely possible if you write from the inside out. Lead with emotion. Show growth. Respect the heart of the practice. Use ChatGPT to support your imagination and clarify what you don't know. And remember—your goal isn't to teach martial arts. Your goal is to tell a story that *feels true*, where the journey through pain, discipline, and purpose hits just as hard as any punch.

Giving Your Protagonist a Fighting Reason

Before your hero throws their first punch, before they tighten their fists or bow on the mat, before they even decide to step into the fight—you have to answer one question: *why are they fighting?* In a martial arts story, this question is everything. It's the emotional engine that powers every scene, every decision, and every moment of growth. A fight without purpose is just noise. But a fight with *meaning*—that's where story lives. And when your protagonist has a clear, compelling reason to fight, your entire narrative becomes more gripping, more grounded, and more unforgettable.

This reason doesn't need to be epic or dramatic. It doesn't have to be about revenge or saving the world. It just has to be personal. It has to matter to *them*. Maybe they're trying to protect someone they love. Maybe they're fighting to redeem themselves after a terrible mistake. Maybe they're searching for identity, peace, or justice. Whatever the reason, it must be strong enough to make them get up after every failure. Strong enough to keep going when everything hurts. Strong enough to risk losing.

A great fighting reason is often tied to something unresolved—grief, guilt, shame, or loss. Maybe your protagonist grew up watching their older brother train, only to see him fall in a match that ended his life. Now they carry that memory like a stone, trying to live up to a legacy they don't fully understand. Or maybe they once froze during a violent confrontation and someone got hurt. Now they train, not just to fight, but to *never freeze again*. These kinds of motivations stay with the audience because they're human. They're not about becoming the strongest—they're about becoming *whole*.

And not all fighting reasons have to come from pain. Maybe your protagonist simply believes in something deeply—a philosophy, a code, a sense of justice. Maybe they fight to prove that martial arts isn't just for the elite. Or to teach others what they once learned from a now-departed master. These motivations are just as powerful because they carry conviction. And conviction is what keeps a story's heart beating.

When you give your protagonist a fighting reason, you also give them a compass. Every scene becomes more focused. They're not just training—they're training *because*. They're not just fighting—they're fighting *for*. That reason should shape how they act in and out of the ring. If they're fighting for redemption, they might hesitate to hurt others. If they're fighting for someone they lost, they might talk to that person in their mind before every match. These small details add weight to their journey and make them more relatable.

It's also okay for your protagonist to *not know* their reason at the start. In fact, that can be part of the arc. Maybe they think they're fighting for glory, but after a crushing defeat, they realize that ego isn't enough. Maybe they think they're fighting to win their master's approval, but later discover they have to fight for themselves. This shift in purpose—this moment of realization—is often what defines the midpoint or climax of a great martial arts story. It's the moment they stop fighting to impress others and start fighting to protect who they are becoming.

You can explore this with ChatGPT by asking, "Give me five reasons a martial arts protagonist might fight that go beyond revenge or fame." Or, "What kind of backstory would drive a character to fight but hate violence?" The answers you get can help shape your entire plot. Once you know the reason, you can build the scenes that test it. You can introduce characters that question it. You can create fights that challenge it.

A good fighting reason also gives you fuel for conflict. What happens when the hero's reason collides with the rival's? What if the hero's fighting to save a dojo while the rival is trying to shut it down for something they believe is just? What if both sides are right in their own way? Now your story has moral complexity. The audience can't just pick a side based on who punches harder—they have to *think* and *feel* their way through it.

And don't forget to show the *cost* of the fight. The reason needs to be strong enough to justify the risks. Is the hero missing school, losing friends, putting their body on the line? Is their family begging them to stop? Are they risking everything for this one thing they believe in? The more real the cost, the more meaningful the reason has to be.

By the time you reach the final showdown, the fighting reason should be crystal clear—not just to the reader, but to the protagonist themselves. Maybe they whisper it under their breath. Maybe they scream it in their opponent's face. Maybe they say nothing at all but show it in every movement. This is the culmination of their arc. It's not just about technique—it's about truth. They're not just fighting to win. They're fighting to *become*.

So when you sit down to write your martial arts story, don't just build the fights. Build the reason. Let it run like a pulse beneath every step your character takes. Let it shape their choices, their fears, their triumphs. Because when the reason is real, the reader feels every blow. And that's when your story stops being just a martial arts tale—and starts becoming something deeply human.

Pacing the Story around Battles and Growth

Writing a martial arts story is about more than just throwing punches on the page—it's about timing. It's about knowing when to hit hard and when to pause. When to break bones and when to break hearts. The rhythm of a good martial arts narrative isn't just a series of fight scenes spaced evenly apart—it's a dance between action and emotion, a flow between external conflict and internal growth. Get the pacing right, and your story becomes a pulse-pounding, emotionally resonant journey. Get it wrong, and you end up with a flat string of sparring matches that don't build to anything meaningful.

So how do you find that rhythm? You start by understanding that every fight must earn its place. Martial arts stories work best when the battles *mean* something. They're never just filler. Each fight needs to push the story forward—by revealing a truth, escalating a rivalry, testing a lesson, or showing who your protagonist is at that moment in their journey. If you approach your pacing with that in mind, you'll naturally space your fight scenes around emotional beats. Growth becomes the thread connecting each punch, kick, and takedown.

A smart way to pace your story is to think in terms of *build-up and payoff.* Your early scenes should introduce the character's current state—flawed, scared, overconfident, lost. Then, as you introduce conflict, use each battle as a test. The first fight might show how unprepared they are. The second might push them beyond their limits. The third might force them to fight someone they don't want to hurt. Each of these scenes should reveal something new about them. That way, you're not just pacing fights—you're pacing *change.*

You can use downtime between battles to explore reflection and growth. After a loss, let the hero spiral—doubt themselves, question their path, lash out at a friend or mentor. After a victory, let them get cocky, or feel the weight of responsibility. These quieter scenes are crucial. They allow readers to *breathe* and connect. They give context to the next clash. Without these spaces, the story becomes noise. With them, it becomes music.

Another way to approach pacing is by varying the scale and stakes of each conflict. Not every fight has to be a life-or-death, knock-down brawl. In fact, your story will feel richer if some battles are internal, others are sparring matches, and a few are emotional confrontations disguised as physical ones. Maybe the hero has to fight their own student. Maybe they fight a rival with no audience, no honor, and no trophy on the line—just unresolved tension and old wounds. These smaller battles can hit just as hard if they're grounded in character.

The key is to make sure every fight is *earned.* Don't throw in a random ambush or street fight just because it's been ten pages since the last one. Instead, ask: what is the emotional goal of this scene? What will the protagonist learn or lose? How will this affect their choices in the next act? You can even ask ChatGPT for help with this pacing logic. Try something like: "Help me outline a martial arts story where each fight reveals a different emotional weakness in the protagonist." You'll get a blueprint for action *and* growth.

Think of your story like a training session. You warm up with lower-stakes moments. Then the pace increases. The pain gets real. The pressure rises. The stakes get higher. And just when it seems like too much—when the hero is about to break—you give them space to recover, reflect, or retreat. Then you hit them again, harder. The climax should feel like the final round in a match that's been building the whole time—not just in terms of fighting, but in terms of who the hero has become.

Another great trick is to echo themes in how you pace scenes. If your story is about balance, alternate your scenes to reflect that—one intense, one quiet. If your story is about chaos, then let the fights come fast and disorienting at first, but gradually slow down as the hero learns control. You're not just pacing for entertainment—you're pacing with purpose.

Supporting characters can also help with pacing. Use them to interrupt, challenge, or reflect the hero's state. A training partner might push too hard, forcing a confrontation. A master might stop a fight to lecture on restraint. A rival might step in with a surprise attack or emotional manipulation. These moments create disruption and tension, which keep the story moving even when there's no literal fight happening.

And don't forget the power of anticipation. Sometimes the *build-up* to a fight is just as compelling as the fight itself. A character preparing for battle, dreading an upcoming match, visualizing their opponent—these scenes build tension and investment. Let your readers *want* the fight before it happens. Make them feel the stakes. Then, when the punches start flying, it hits harder.

Use ChatGPT to structure this rhythm. You can prompt: "Build a pacing outline for a martial arts story with emotional peaks after each fight," or "Design a story where every third chapter includes a physical or emotional battle." With just a few tweaks, you can fine-tune the flow so that nothing drags and nothing overwhelms.

In the end, pacing your story around battles and growth means recognizing that the best fights are always tied to character. They're not just choreography—they're turning points. So space them out wisely. Let each one say something new. Use the time in between to build emotion, deepen the journey, and raise the stakes. That's how you write a martial arts story that doesn't just fight well—but *flows* like a true warrior.

Weaving Real Techniques into Fiction

In a martial arts story, using real techniques is like adding seasoning to a dish—it's not everything, but it makes the flavor richer. Authenticity gives your fights a tactile edge, grounding the action and inviting readers into a world that feels both believable and exciting. But the goal isn't to write a technical manual or overwhelm your audience with jargon—it's to *weave* those real techniques into the emotional, visual, and narrative fabric of your story. You're not trying to impress martial arts experts—you're trying to create a story that *feels* real, even to someone who's never stepped on a mat.

So how do you do that, especially if you're not a martial artist yourself? You start with understanding what the technique *does* in the scene, and more importantly, what it *means*. A throw, a lock, a strike—they all carry narrative weight depending on how and when they're used. A clean, efficient wrist lock might show control and discipline. A frantic barrage of punches might show desperation. A chokehold that ends a fight in silence might say more about a character's restraint—or lack of it—than any amount of dialogue.

To get the terminology and mechanics right, use ChatGPT as your sparring partner. You can ask, "What's a good takedown from Judo that would work in a close-range street fight?" or "Describe a Wing Chun technique that focuses on centerline control." You'll get clean, digestible descriptions that you can adapt to the tone and flow of your story. From there, you don't have to go into encyclopedic detail. Just *suggest* the movement. Let the reader feel the force, the speed, the crack of contact.

Here's the secret: real techniques work best in fiction when they're part of the *character*. A cautious fighter might favor defensive moves like blocks, parries, and evasion. A bruiser might go for body shots and slams. A master might use minimal effort with maximum effect. Choose techniques that reflect your characters' personalities, emotional states, and philosophies. You can even show character development through changing techniques. Maybe your hero starts off swinging wildly and later learns to fight with calm precision, using clean footwork and controlled strikes. That's growth—told through movement.

You also want to match technique to setting. A spinning back kick looks fantastic in a wide-open tournament ring but makes no sense in a cramped hallway. A ground grappling sequence might be tense and tactical in a one-on-one alley fight but awkward and risky in a crowded market. Let the environment influence what's possible. Ask yourself, "What would a trained fighter do *here*?" Not what looks cool—but what feels right. That realism is what turns a good scene into a great one.

Another trick is to layer technique with emotion. Maybe the hero remembers being taught a move as a child by someone they lost. When they finally use it, it's not just effective—it's *symbolic*. Maybe they swore never to use a certain technique because of what it represents—but now, with everything on the line, they break that promise. These moments hit hard because the technique isn't just physical. It's narrative. It's loaded.

You don't need to overwhelm the reader with constant technique callouts, either. In fact, sometimes it's better to be subtle. You can say, "He slipped past the guard and swept her legs with a sudden low rotation," without needing to name the exact Judo throw. But when you *do* want to name a move—"He launched into a double-leg takedown"—make sure the context is clear. A quick line explaining how it works or what it accomplishes keeps the reader grounded. You can say, "He shot low, arms around both thighs, and slammed his opponent to the mat before they could sprawl," and even non-martial artists will feel the impact.

And when a specific martial art is part of your character's identity, the way they fight should express that style's rhythm and tactics. A Taekwondo fighter might be bouncing, looking for range and timing high kicks. A Muay Thai striker will be tight, centered, and deadly with elbows and knees. A Brazilian Jiu-Jitsu fighter wants the fight on the ground. You don't need to constantly remind the reader what art they're using—just let the movement show it. Use cues in the way they move, the way they stand, the way they control space.

You can also use ChatGPT to blend realism with originality. Try asking, "Create a fictional martial arts style based on snake movements, using real-world grappling techniques," or "Give me five unique combinations of strikes and sweeps a Shaolin-style fighter might use." You'll get material that's grounded in real technique but creatively fresh—perfect for fiction that feels authentic without being dry.

Fight choreography in a novel is very different from on-screen. You're not just showing who kicks who—you're painting rhythm, emotion, and tension. You want scenes to have pace. A slow build. A clash. A moment of struggle. A reversal. A breath. A final move. When real techniques are woven into that rhythm, they enhance it rather than interrupt it. So don't treat them like trivia—treat them like brushstrokes.

And don't worry if you're still learning as you write. Even seasoned writers ask for help when describing action. You can always say, "Help me write a short fight scene where my protagonist uses a defensive stance to avoid punches and finishes with a low sweep," and ChatGPT will generate something clean and adaptable that you can customize to your characters and tone.

Ultimately, real techniques in fiction aren't about being impressive. They're about grounding your story, enriching your characters, and giving the reader a sense that what's happening on the page could really happen—because it comes from something true. Weaving those moves into your narrative with meaning, emotion, and flow is what brings your martial arts story to life.

So research a little. Ask for help. Choose techniques that *say something*. Then throw them into your story with style, restraint, and a strong emotional punch. Because the best martial arts fiction doesn't just move. It *hits*.

Dialogue that Echoes Like a Strike

In martial arts stories, fists may carry the weight of justice, revenge, or redemption—but sometimes a single *line of dialogue* can land harder than any punch. The right words, spoken at the right time, can rattle a rival, define a character, or even *change the course of a fight*. Martial arts fiction thrives on restraint, rhythm, and intensity—and your dialogue should reflect that. Just like a strike, it needs timing, intent, and clarity. And when delivered with precision, it doesn't just fill space—it *echoes*.

Think about the way martial artists move: deliberate, minimal, purposeful. That's how their dialogue should feel. You don't need long speeches or heavy exposition. In fact, the best lines are often short, loaded, and open to interpretation. "You're not ready." "I taught you that move." "This ends when you stop running." These aren't just words. They're weapons. They cut deep because they carry history, subtext, and emotional weight.

So how do you craft dialogue that hits like a strike? You start by understanding who's speaking and *why* they're speaking. In a martial arts story, characters often speak less—but when they do, it counts. The mentor uses silence to teach. The rival uses words to provoke. The hero may not know what to say until they've been through the fire. Let that be reflected in their tone. A student might speak with too much confidence early on, only to grow quieter as they gain understanding. A master might say little—but when they do, their words land like a final blow.

Each line should *reveal* something—about belief, emotion, or philosophy. Think about the core values of your characters. What do they believe about strength? About honor? About themselves? When these values are tested, their dialogue becomes more than conversation—it becomes a reflection of their journey. Maybe your protagonist starts out saying things like, "I'm going to be the best," but by the end, they're saying, "I just want to be better than who I was." That shift shows growth. It shows that the fight is no longer about proving something to others—but understanding something within.

Silence is just as important as speech. Martial arts stories are full of moments where characters say nothing at all—and that's often where the real dialogue lives. The refusal to respond. The long stare after a defeat. The hesitation before accepting a challenge. Let your characters *breathe*. Let them say less so the reader listens more. If a character says only one sentence in a scene, make it *sting*.

A great trick is to let dialogue *mirror action*. Maybe your character learns a lesson in the ring that echoes something a master said earlier. "A clenched fist can't catch anything." At the time, it sounded like nonsense. But now, in the middle of a fight, they remember it—and apply it. That callback makes the moment satisfying. The line comes full circle, like a well-thrown boomerang returning to the hand.

Let your antagonist have sharp lines too. The best villains don't just fight dirty—they *speak* dirty. They twist the truth. They press on emotional wounds. "You'll always be second best." "You don't even know why you're fighting." "Your master died knowing you'd fail." Cold, cruel lines that do more damage than a roundhouse. The protagonist's response—whether they speak back or *don't*—says everything.

With ChatGPT, you can develop dialogue fast by feeding it the tone you want. Try, "Give me five short lines a martial arts master might say to a student about patience," or "Write an intense exchange between a martial arts protagonist and their rival before the final fight." Then refine it, shape it, make it yours. Look for the sentence that gives you a chill. That's the one you keep.

And don't forget: repetition can be a weapon. A line spoken early in the story can come back with new meaning later. Maybe a mentor always said, "Feet first, heart second." When the student says it in the final fight, it carries history, respect, and closure. The same line, repeated in a new context, becomes something else entirely. That's how dialogue echoes.

Use contrast in tone. Maybe your protagonist is emotionally raw, while their opponent is cold and composed. Or vice versa. That friction adds tension. It's the verbal equivalent of two stances squaring off. A fight scene doesn't have to begin with punches—it can begin with a single whispered threat. One line that drops into the silence like a stone in water.

Even humor has a place, but it should be razor-sharp. A sarcastic student. A dry-witted master. A rival who taunts with deadly calm. Just make sure it never undercuts the tension unless that's the point. In martial arts stories, humor often lands best when it's used sparingly—right before the storm.

And when the final fight comes, don't drown it in words. Let the punches speak. But allow a line—one line—to rise above the sound of fists and breathing. Something honest. Something earned. Something that lingers. Maybe it's a surrender. Maybe it's forgiveness. Maybe it's a challenge. That last line before the final blow should feel like a sword drawn from its sheath—inevitable and precise.

Because in martial arts fiction, when the fight ends, readers may not remember every move—but they will remember what was said.

So write your dialogue like you're throwing strikes. With focus. With purpose. With impact. Let it move with the same rhythm as a kata. Let it carry silence in its pauses, power in its brevity, and truth in its timing. That's how you make it echo. That's how you make it *hurt*.

Finding the Soul of the Martial Arts Tale

Beneath the kicks, the clashes, the breathless duels and brutal takedowns, there's something quiet and unshakable that makes a martial arts story resonate—it's the *soul*. It's the heartbeat of the tale. The part that isn't found in technique or tournament brackets, but in *why* we train, *why* we fight, and *why* we stop. Without that soul, a martial arts story is just choreography. With it, the story transforms into something timeless, something human. When you find the soul of your story, every punch lands deeper, every scar matters more, and every choice made by your characters echoes long after the final blow.

The soul of a martial arts tale often lives in the *quiet moments*. The stillness before the storm. The bowed heads. The solitary training under rain. The hesitant hand reaching out to help a fallen opponent. It's the space between action where intention lives. It's in the ritual of binding one's fists before a match—not for show, but as a silent promise to fight with purpose. When you slow down enough to notice these moments, your story begins to breathe with meaning.

At its core, martial arts fiction is about *transformation*. Not just of the body, but of the spirit. A good story doesn't ask, "Can they win the fight?" It asks, "Who are they becoming through this fight?" Your protagonist might begin angry, scared, arrogant, or aimless—but over the course of the story, they're forged into something more. Stronger not because they hit harder, but because they understand themselves. The soul of your story is in *that understanding*.

The martial arts tale also thrives on *values*. Honor. Discipline. Mercy. Self-awareness. These aren't just lofty ideals—they're the decisions your characters are constantly forced to make. Does your hero show mercy or seek revenge? Do they fight for justice or for glory? Do they listen to their master or follow their own path? These choices give your story spiritual shape. They turn simple fights into moral and emotional crossroads. And that's where readers lean in—not just to see who wins, but to see who *they* would be in that same moment.

You also find the soul in *legacy*. Who taught the hero? What was passed down—wisdom, trauma, responsibility? Martial arts are rarely practiced in isolation. Every movement carries the echo of someone who came before. Maybe the hero is trying to honor a mentor. Maybe they're trying to break free from a toxic tradition. Maybe they're rebuilding something sacred that was lost. These storylines give your tale depth, generational weight, and emotional continuity.

Don't be afraid to explore *stillness*. Martial arts is as much about the space between strikes as the strikes themselves. Your character may fight their greatest battle not with their fists, but sitting alone after a loss, remembering what it felt like to fail someone they loved. Or facing their rival outside of the ring and choosing not to fight at all. These moments of restraint, reflection, and choice are where the soul of the story glows brightest.

You can also think of the soul as a question your story is trying to answer. Not a plot question, like "Will they win the tournament?" but a thematic one like, "What does it mean to fight with honor?" or "Can violence ever lead to peace?" or "Is strength found in control, or in letting go?" This question can guide your scenes, your character arcs, and your fights. It's the invisible thread that pulls everything together, even when the story takes wild turns or brutal detours.

And your setting can carry soul too. The dojo that's falling apart but still sacred. The forest clearing where the hero trains alone. The chalk lines drawn on the floor of a prison cell as a makeshift ring. These places hold memory, weight, and emotion. Describe them with more than just visual detail—infuse them with feeling. Let the reader *sense* the spirit of these places, not just *see* them.

Use your supporting characters to reveal the soul of the story. The student who trains even when no one's watching. The rival who secretly envies the hero's restraint. The master who teaches not through force, but silence. These characters don't need long arcs—they just need *truth*. One gesture, one line of dialogue, one story from their past can light up the deeper themes of your narrative.

And don't forget to turn inward when writing. What would *you* fight for? What lesson do *you* keep relearning? The martial arts story is personal—not just for the character, but for the writer. You don't need to have studied Kung Fu to write something powerful. You just need to have struggled. To have changed. To have stood up after a fall. That's the spirit of martial arts. And that's what readers connect with.

ChatGPT can help you explore these inner layers. You can ask, "What's a philosophical question to explore in a martial arts story?" or "Describe a quiet, emotional scene between a master and student that reveals a deeper theme." You'll get moments and ideas you can fold into your existing structure—moments that anchor your fights with something richer than impact.

In the end, the soul of the martial arts tale is found in contrast—between stillness and motion, tradition and change, discipline and emotion. It's the journey from chaos to clarity. From anger to control. From survival to meaning.

So as you write, look beyond the moves. Look for the *why* behind the punch. The *quiet* after the scream. The decision not to strike. That's where your story lives. That's where its spirit breathes. That's where readers stop and say, "That hit me." Not just on the page—but in the heart.

Writing the First Page with a Gripping Movement

Your first page is your first punch—it's what pulls the reader in, sets the tone, and says, "This is a story worth following." And in martial arts fiction, opening with *movement*—a moment of action, tension, or internal energy—can be the perfect way to grab hold of your reader and never let go. But that doesn't mean launching into a full-on fight scene right away. Movement doesn't always mean fists flying. It can be the flick of a wrist, the snap of a belt, the stillness before a strike, or even the tension of a breath held too long. What matters is that it *pulls*.

A great martial arts story doesn't begin with explanation. It begins with intention. Something happening, or about to happen. Someone in motion—physically, emotionally, spiritually. A student on the verge of giving up. A rival watching silently from the back of the dojo. A fist pausing mid-air before it lands. That *moment* is where your reader steps into the story, heart already racing, questions already forming. They don't need the history of the dojo or the complete backstory of the protagonist just yet. What they need is to *feel* something happening.

Imagine opening on a training hall lit only by sunrise. A lone figure performs a kata—every move fluid, sharp, graceful. And then they stop, staring at the empty doorway where someone who used to watch them no longer stands. No dialogue. No exposition. Just *movement* filled with meaning. That's an opening page that breathes. That sets up emotion, mystery, and tone all at once.

Or maybe you open on the sounds of a crowded underground fight—cheering, blood hitting the mat, boots stomping the cage. But the camera doesn't follow the fighters. It follows someone in the crowd, quiet, tense, watching. Not because they enjoy the violence—but because they've been *called back* to it. Now your story has atmosphere, immediacy, and tension without a single paragraph of backstory.

Even a quiet opening can carry gripping motion. Think of a character seated in seiza, staring at a single candle's flame. The door opens. A note slides across the floor. The candle flickers as the wind follows. We don't know who the character is. We don't know what the note says. But we're already *inside* the story, wondering what will come next.

This is where ChatGPT can be a powerful ally. Ask it: "Write a first page for a martial arts story that opens with a moment of stillness before a surprise attack," or "Give me a powerful first scene where a student is training alone and remembers their master's last words." You'll get raw material to sculpt into something personal and strong.

Don't be afraid to write your first page like a poem. Short lines. Strong images. Crisp motion. You're not trying to explain everything—you're trying to *invite*. Let the first paragraph create questions, tension, and mood. Is this person training? Waiting? Running? Hiding? Let that uncertainty carry the reader forward.

Consider writing the opening like the start of a match. The space between the bow and the first move. That charged stillness. The air tight with potential. That's what you want your reader to feel. That something is coming, and they *have* to see what it is.

You can also frame your opening around a *philosophical idea*, wrapped in movement. A master once said, "The first strike is not with the body, but with the will." Then show a character who's afraid to throw a punch—not because they're weak, but because they know what that punch means. Now you've got movement, theme, and psychology layered in a single line.

Most of all, *trust the moment*. Don't rush to explain. Let the action or stillness speak. If you open on a fight, let the blows reflect character—reckless, focused, scared, angry. If you open on training, let us see the ritual. If you open on stillness, let it be heavy with memory.

And remember—this is a martial arts story. It's about control, tension, and flow. Your first page should *move* like your story will. Not loud without meaning. Not fast without rhythm. But with *presence*. With clarity. With intent.

Because when your first page moves with that kind of grace, readers don't just see the story. They *feel* it. And they stay. Ready for the next strike. Ready for the next step. Ready for the journey.

Testing Your Fight Scenes for Rhythm and Impact

Writing a good fight scene is like composing music—you're dealing with timing, tempo, emotional beats, and crescendos of energy. And in martial arts fiction, where combat is often the centerpiece of the story, your fight scenes need more than just accuracy and action. They need *rhythm* that keeps the reader turning pages and *impact* that makes them feel every blow, block, and breath. If a fight scene drags, it loses momentum. If it's all motion and no emotion, it falls flat. So how do you test your fight scenes to make sure they sing with rhythm and hit with real force?

Start by asking yourself this: does the fight *build*? Like a good song or scene, a great fight shouldn't feel like it starts at full volume. There should be a beginning—usually tense, measured, uncertain. Then escalation. A shift. A surprise. And finally, a moment of clarity or transformation that punctuates the scene. This doesn't mean every fight has to be epic or long. Even a short skirmish should have a beginning, middle, and end. If the action feels like a flat line—just punch-punch-kick without change—it's not a fight, it's a list.

You can test this by *reading your scene aloud*. Rhythm lives in the sentences. Short, choppy lines build speed and urgency. Longer, more descriptive lines slow things down and allow for reflection. If the whole scene is written in long, meandering sentences, it may feel sluggish. If it's all one-liners, it may lack depth. Mix it up. Use sentence structure to mirror the movement. A sudden break in rhythm—like a single-word paragraph—can land like a strike if timed well.

Also test for *emotional clarity*. Ask yourself: do I know what my character is feeling at each stage of the fight? Fear? Focus? Fury? Restraint? A fight is never just physical—it's emotional. Does the character hesitate before striking someone they care about? Do they flinch remembering a past injury? Do they lose control? These moments give the fight meaning beyond physical choreography. If a reader knows *why* the character fights, every move means more.

You can run a simple test: remove the fight and replace it with dialogue. Does the *emotional arc* still hold up? If the answer is yes, you've got something layered. If the answer is no, you may need to inject more subtext and conflict into the physicality.

Impact also depends on *specificity*. "He punched him in the face" is okay, but "He drove his knuckles into the soft spot just below the eye, and felt the cartilage crunch" hits harder. Use sensory detail—but sparingly. You don't need to describe every finger placement or bone. Just the right moment. The right detail. The breath knocked out. The mat under their back. The silence after the final blow. These are the beats that land.

Pacing within a fight scene matters too. Break up the combat with moments of pause—an exchanged look, a circling breath, a memory flashing through the mind. These pauses reset the tempo and allow the next sequence to feel fresh. Non-stop fighting gets dull fast. Well-timed pauses keep readers alert and emotionally engaged.

Let the setting play a role. Are they slipping in the rain? Ducking behind dojo pillars? Trapped in a tight stairwell? Environmental interaction keeps the rhythm unpredictable. It also increases realism and tension. And readers love when a character uses their surroundings in a clever way—turning a training weapon into a surprise tactic, or using a wall to execute a kick with more force.

You can also run a "reader reaction" test using ChatGPT. Prompt: "Read this fight scene and tell me if the rhythm feels too fast, too slow, or just right," or "Where can I add more emotional impact in this sequence?" You'll get honest, targeted feedback instantly—and that's gold when polishing high-intensity scenes on a tight writing schedule.

A big part of rhythm is knowing when to *end* the scene. Don't overstay your welcome. A fight should end either with a clear winner, an interruption, or a major shift in stakes. If you keep it going just because you like the choreography, it might start to feel indulgent. Look for that natural stopping point—usually when something changes: someone falls, someone chooses not to strike, someone says something that silences everything.

Try the "last hit test." Does your final line land like a strike? Maybe it's a line of dialogue. Maybe it's a final blow. Maybe it's the sound of the crowd, or the breath the hero didn't realize they were holding. That line should be a *cliff, not a fade*. Something that lets the reader feel the aftermath, even after they've turned the page.

Remember: rhythm and impact are not just about violence. They're about *storytelling*. Your fights should reveal character. Transform relationships. Raise stakes. Resolve—or deepen—emotional arcs. When you test your fight scenes for these elements, you're not just fixing pacing. You're forging the very core of the narrative in heat and motion.

So step back. Read it aloud. Feel the flow. Track the emotion. Mark the high points. Breathe with your character. And when the rhythm is right, you won't just have written a fight—you'll have written a *moment*. One that strikes, lingers, and *echoes*.

Creating the Master: Mentor Characters That Matter

The martial arts master is one of the most iconic and beloved figures in storytelling. Whether they're a grizzled old sensei in a faded robe, a silent wanderer who teaches with glances, or a no-nonsense coach who believes pain is a lesson, the mentor isn't just there to pass down knowledge—they're the soul of the story. When written well, they become more than a supporting role. They become the moral compass, the emotional spine, and the shadow the protagonist must either follow—or outgrow. And if you want your martial arts tale to resonate, your master character needs to *matter*.

The first thing to understand is that the master isn't just there to teach technique. Sure, they can demonstrate a deadly form or help the hero perfect a strike, but their real job is to challenge the protagonist's beliefs. A good master doesn't simply hand out wisdom—they force the student to *earn it*. They provoke change. They make the hero uncomfortable. They confront the flaws the hero doesn't want to see. That's what makes them powerful—and unforgettable.

Start by asking: *what does your master believe in?* Every good mentor in a martial arts story is a vessel for philosophy. Maybe they believe that restraint is the highest form of strength. Or that fighting is a form of prayer. Or that there's no such thing as winning—only surviving with dignity. Whatever their worldview, it should be clear, personal, and challenged through the story. If the student accepts it, they carry the legacy forward. If they reject it, the conflict deepens. Either way, the philosophy creates tension, structure, and soul.

Also consider the *flaws* in your master. The best mentor characters are never perfect. Maybe they failed a former student. Maybe they've stopped fighting for something they once believed in. Maybe they're so committed to the code that they can't adapt. These cracks in their armor create powerful dynamics. The student sees them as infallible—until they don't. And when that moment comes, it's not just a plot twist. It's a turning point in the hero's emotional journey.

There's also the question of *tone*. Not every master needs to be the wise old monk. You can create a hot-headed, unorthodox teacher who breaks every rule but gets results. Or a calm, quiet figure who speaks in riddles that only make sense after the final fight. Or even a reluctant mentor who never wanted to teach but was pulled into it out of guilt, duty, or love. The tone of your master sets the emotional frequency of your training scenes and helps define the culture of your dojo or world.

If you're looking to generate fresh ideas, ask ChatGPT for help. Try a prompt like, "Create a martial arts master who trains students through silence and unconventional tasks," or "Give me a mentor character who lost a student in a fight and now trains with fear." You'll be given depth, backstory, and potential dialogue—all of which you can develop further to serve your narrative.

A good master character also needs to *earn the reader's respect*. They don't have to win every fight or dominate the dojo, but they should have moments that show why they matter. Maybe they defuse a fight without throwing a single punch. Maybe they stop the hero mid-training with just a look. Maybe they tell a story from their past that reframes the entire conflict. These moments give the master their own arc and identity. They're not just background—they're legacy in motion.

Think about how the master *teaches*. Do they rely on drills and repetition? Do they set tasks with hidden lessons, like telling a student to carry water every day to build discipline? Do they spar directly, offering wisdom through pain and pressure? These teaching methods reveal not only the master's values, but also their emotional state. A bitter master might teach through punishment. A hopeful one through encouragement. The method is the message.

And don't forget the *exit strategy*. Most mentor figures eventually leave the story—whether through death, departure, or being surpassed by the student. How that exit happens is often one of the most emotional moments in a martial arts narrative. Maybe they die protecting the student. Maybe they walk away after seeing the student rise. Maybe they stand beside the student at the end, proud but silent. However it happens, the ending of the mentor's arc should feel earned and reflective of everything they stood for.

If you want to test the emotional impact of your master character, ask yourself: *What would the story lose without them?* If the answer is "not much," then it's time to dig deeper. Make them challenge the hero. Make them stand for something. Make them *teach* in every sense of the word—through words, actions, mistakes, and sacrifice.

And if you're writing a one-day draft and need speed, ask ChatGPT for dialogue or emotional turning points: "Write a scene where a martial arts master finally praises their student after years of silence," or "Create a training scene that shows the master breaking their own rule." These moments can become some of the most powerful in your book.

In the end, creating a mentor that matters means going beyond tropes. It means building someone who *knows*, who *hurts*, who *teaches*, and who *changes* others just by being there. Because long after the final match is fought, readers remember the hand that helped the hero stand. The voice that taught them to breathe. And the presence that reminded them that strength isn't always shown in battle—but in the choice to rise, again and again.

That's the master's gift. That's their legacy. And that's what makes them unforgettable.

Using ChatGPT to Brainstorm Epic Battles

There's something magnetic about an epic martial arts battle—the kind that makes your heart race just reading it. Whether it's a long-awaited final showdown between rivals, a battle atop a burning pagoda, or a desperate last stand in the pouring rain, these scenes are where everything you've built comes to life. But writing them, especially under a time crunch or creative pressure, can feel overwhelming. That's where ChatGPT becomes your secret weapon—a sparring partner that never tires, full of creative energy and cinematic instinct. When you know how to prompt it, ChatGPT can help you brainstorm and shape an unforgettable martial arts battle that doesn't just dazzle—it *means something*.

First, you'll want to start with the big picture. Before you dive into punches and kicks, clarify the purpose of the battle. What's at stake emotionally and narratively? Is this a final test, a personal reckoning, or a symbolic confrontation of old beliefs? Once you know *why* the fight matters, you can guide ChatGPT to deliver options that reinforce the emotional core. Try prompting:

"Give me three epic martial arts battle ideas that resolve a story about redemption and lost honor."

In return, you'll get ideas that are already embedded with character conflict and meaning, not just action choreography.

Then, narrow the scope and focus on location. Setting adds tension, mood, and opportunity for creative movement. A mountain pass creates narrow footwork. A crumbling dojo becomes symbolic as tradition literally falls apart. A rooftop at dawn invites poetic visuals. Prompt ChatGPT with something like:

"Describe an atmospheric setting for a one-on-one martial arts duel that feels emotional and symbolic."

This gives you a sensory foundation—a stage worthy of the fight—and helps shape the battle's tone before the first strike is thrown.

From there, focus on the fighters. Who's involved? What are their styles? What do they fear, hope, or hide? What has changed in them since their last confrontation? These questions guide the choreography toward storytelling. Instead of just, "He kicked, she blocked," you'll get, "She slipped under his spinning kick, the same one that broke her jaw two years ago—and this time, she didn't flinch." Use prompts like:

"Write a brief character-based martial arts fight between a student and their former master, filled with emotional tension and symbolic moves."

This turns the fight into a narrative. Every movement reflects a lesson, a betrayal, or a transformation.

You can also ask ChatGPT to help *structure* the fight for maximum impact. A good battle has rhythm and shifts in momentum. Early hesitation. Sudden bursts. Tactical retreats. A reversal. A mistake. A turning point. You can prompt:

"Outline the five major beats of an epic martial arts duel where the underdog wins by embracing their master's forgotten philosophy."

This gives you a framework to build your scene with peaks, valleys, and emotional highs. It turns chaos into structure—without losing the thrill.

Want help with choreography? ChatGPT can invent combinations of real and fictional moves that feel fresh and visual. Try:

"Give me a three-move combo for a grounded, patient fighter versus an aggressive, acrobatic opponent."

Now you're shaping a dance of personalities, not just techniques. You'll also get ideas for counters, surprise tactics, and terrain-based maneuvers that you may not have thought of on your own.

Don't forget about dialogue. An epic battle isn't just about movement—it's about the *words* that land just as hard. Ask:

"Write a few short lines of intense dialogue between two fighters mid-duel, touching on betrayal and forgiveness."

The right line in the middle of a fight can elevate the moment, remind us what's at stake, or reveal a truth that has nothing to do with who's stronger.

If your battle includes multiple fighters—say, a tournament brawl or a battle royale—ChatGPT can help you manage the chaos. Prompt with:

"Create a martial arts tournament quarterfinal with four distinct fighters, each using a different fighting style and personality, all leading to one emerging victor."

You'll get a breakdown of styles, strengths, and conflict points, which can then be woven into fast-paced, character-driven action.

And if you're writing on a tight schedule, let ChatGPT help you fill in sensory details on the fly. Ask for sights, sounds, smells, even internal monologue. Something like:

"Describe the feeling of a martial artist realizing mid-fight that they've surpassed their teacher."

This injects emotion between the strikes, making the moment land harder than any uppercut.

When your draft is done, you can even test it with a final prompt:

"Read this fight scene and tell me if the rhythm flows and where I can increase tension or emotion."

ChatGPT becomes your editor, pointing out slow spots, missed emotional beats, or places where an extra breath—or a final blow—could make all the difference.

In short, using ChatGPT to brainstorm epic battles isn't about handing over the creative wheel—it's about inviting a relentless creative partner into your corner. You provide the vision, the theme, the arc—and ChatGPT gives you sparks, structure, and surprise.

Because the best martial arts battles aren't remembered for how hard they hit. They're remembered for *why* they happened. For who stood up. Who fell down. And who walked away changed. With ChatGPT in your corner, you can build that kind of fight—one strike, one heartbeat, one scene at a time.

Designing a Martial Arts World with Cultural Depth

Designing a martial arts world with real cultural depth is like crafting a living organism—it breathes, it grows, and it holds a memory of everyone who's moved through it. It's more than just choosing where the story happens or which martial art is practiced. It's about *why* people fight, *what* they believe, and *how* culture, tradition, honor, and philosophy shape every aspect of their lives. If you're building a martial arts world from scratch—or reimagining the real one through fiction—the depth you give to the culture around combat will transform your story from simple action to meaningful mythology.

So where do you start? Not with punches. Not with tournaments. You start with *values*. What does this world believe about strength? Is strength revered? Feared? Is combat seen as divine, criminal, sacred, or sport? These beliefs set the tone for your entire world. In some cultures, warriors might be treated as spiritual leaders. In others, fighters may be outcasts. Maybe martial arts is tightly regulated by a ruling order. Maybe it's a forbidden legacy kept alive by secret schools in the mountains. Ask yourself: *How does society view those who fight?* That answer gives your story purpose.

From there, you build the *philosophy* of martial practice. Most real-world martial arts are tied to cultural concepts—Bushido in Japan, Tao in Chinese traditions, the warrior monks of Thailand, the ritual dances of Capoeira in Brazil. Even modern systems like MMA carry cultural weight, blending global traditions with commercial spectacle. When designing your world, ask: what do practitioners of this art believe? Is it about discipline over dominance? Does it connect to nature, spirit, or community? Or is it used to control, to rule, to suppress? This internal philosophy will affect the tone of your battles and the shape of your characters' internal arcs.

Now layer in the *traditions*. Do students bow before stepping into the ring? Are there uniforms, titles, oaths? Are certain colors sacred? Do schools burn incense, recite mantras, trace tattoos before a match? Traditions bring texture. They remind the reader that this isn't just a fighting style—it's a *culture*. Even invented customs can feel deeply authentic if they're tied to emotional meaning. Maybe every warrior carves their lineage into a stone wall after their first real victory. Maybe broken weapons are buried, not discarded. Maybe silence after a match is the highest form of respect. These moments are what make a fictional world feel alive.

Then think about the *settings*. A martial arts world isn't just about where people fight—it's about how the environment reflects the culture. If your story takes place in a desert kingdom, maybe fighters move like wind and sand—slow to build, devastating when released. If your world is built around mountains, perhaps fighters train at high altitudes, balancing on narrow cliffs, drawing breath like monks. Urban settings can shift the tone—underground rings, rooftop battles, spiritual dojos hidden behind bodegas or tea shops. Let the world's physical layout mirror the belief systems and traditions of the fighters who inhabit it.

Use *architecture* to show history. A crumbling dojo might be all that's left of a once-revered warrior class. A bloodstained arena might be the site of a rebellion long suppressed. A statue of a forgotten master at the village gates can speak louder than exposition ever could. Don't just describe places—*use them to tell your story*.

You'll also want to establish *conflicts* that are born out of culture. Maybe rival schools interpret a sacred text differently and have trained for centuries to destroy one another. Maybe a reformist movement wants to break the old systems, while traditionalists cling to the past. Maybe there's a political regime trying to control martial knowledge, limiting who gets to learn—and who stays powerless. These cultural tensions make your story feel like it has weight, history, and consequences.

The *language* of your martial arts world can reinforce culture too. What do they call their students? Their enemies? Their masters? Do they have words that carry layered meanings—like a term that means both "defeat" and "humility"? Maybe the highest rank isn't called "master," but something like "the Empty One"—someone who has let go of ego. Small linguistic choices can add depth and emotional texture.

Let's not forget *mythology*. Every martial arts culture needs legends. The first warrior. The forbidden technique. The unbeatable style lost to time. Maybe there's a story of a fighter who stopped a war with a single movement—or who burned down their own school to protect its teachings. These myths can influence your characters' beliefs, motivations, and fears. Even if they don't know whether the stories are true, they *act* as if they are—and that shapes their path.

And yes, ChatGPT can help you build all of this. You can prompt:

"Create a fictional martial arts culture based on wind and shadows, with a focus on silent movement and honor through restraint."

Or ask:

"Describe five martial rituals practiced in a society where combat is considered a sacred language."

You'll get full ideas, names, techniques, traditions, and philosophies that you can tweak and make your own.

Finally, tie the culture to the *emotional journey* of your characters. Maybe your protagonist begins by chasing power because the culture idolizes it—but slowly learns that true strength lies in balance. Maybe they were raised by a brutal school and must now unlearn everything they were taught. Maybe they're the only one willing to break an ancient tradition to save someone. When your world's cultural depth becomes personal to the characters, the story starts to glow from the inside.

So don't just build a place where people fight. Build a world where people *believe*. Where every movement is part of a greater language. Where combat is legacy. Where history, tradition, and tension shape every story beat like a well-thrown strike.

That's when your martial arts world becomes more than fiction—it becomes a myth in motion.

Writing for Screen vs. Writing for Novel

Martial arts stories are inherently visual—full of motion, rhythm, tension, and transformation. That's why they've thrived on screen, from the sweeping choreography of classic kung fu films to the raw intimacy of modern fight dramas. But they've also found life in novels, where emotion and inner struggle can be explored more deeply, and action is as much about *why* as *how*. If you're writing martial arts fiction, understanding the key differences between writing for screen and writing for the page will help you shape your story for the right medium—or adapt it between the two with purpose and impact.

Let's start with the **visual nature of screenwriting**. When you're writing a martial arts screenplay, you're thinking in images. The camera is your eyes. You don't tell the audience what the character is feeling unless you *show* it through their actions, expressions, or dialogue. A screenwriter doesn't say, "He was nervous before the fight." Instead, they write, "He bounces on the balls of his feet, fingers twitching, eyes darting toward the exit." Emotion is shown in *behavior*, not description.

Screenwriting is also **lean and minimalist**. A script is a blueprint, not a novel. You want short, punchy action lines. Clear, concise direction. Dialogue that feels real but tight. There's no room for internal monologue unless you're using voiceover—and even then, it's used sparingly. Every page roughly equals one minute of screen time, so a fight scene that takes three pages better be three minutes of intense, dynamic choreography, not a blow-by-blow diary.

In a **novel**, however, you have the luxury of space. You can dive into the character's thoughts mid-fight. You can slow down time. You can explore the philosophy behind a strike or the memory a technique brings back. The prose can linger, circle, reveal. Instead of seeing the twitch in the hero's hand, you can describe the *meaning* behind that twitch—the trauma it's linked to, the fear it hides, the vow it reflects. In a novel, *you are the camera*, the editor, and the sound designer, all at once.

In screenwriting, **structure is law**. Three acts. Inciting incident by page ten. Midpoint twist. Climax in the final ten pages. While novels can be more fluid with structure, martial arts stories often benefit from a similar framework, especially if action is central. But you don't have to hit the same beats at the same speed. In a novel, a training montage might be ten pages of growth, introspection, and symbolic movement. On screen, it's thirty seconds with a soundtrack and fast cuts. Both have emotional weight—but the **delivery is different**.

Dialogue is another key difference. In scripts, dialogue must carry the story and reveal character without dragging. It needs rhythm and intent. In novels, dialogue can breathe. You can insert pauses, thoughts, reactions, subtext layered through internal narration. You can let the words sit beside memory, fear, or hope. The same line—"You're not ready"—reads one way on screen, but in a novel, it might be followed by an entire paragraph about how the protagonist *knows* the speaker is right, and hates them for it.

Action scenes in screenplays are written for *choreographers and directors*. You might say, "They exchange a flurry of blows—each faster than the last—until he lands a clean spinning elbow." That's enough. The stunt team and director will bring it to life. In a novel, you're the one bringing it to life. You describe the *weight* of the elbow, the *sound* of the contact, the *shock* in the opponent's eyes, the *blood* on the floor. You're not just showing the move—you're making the reader *feel* it.

With ChatGPT, you can explore both forms easily. Ask, "Write this martial arts scene as a screenplay," or "Now rewrite that same scene as a novel passage with internal emotion." You'll see how tone, rhythm, and detail shift. Use this to experiment, compare, and figure out which format suits your story—or how to *adapt one into the other*.

One major storytelling shift comes with **point of view**. Novels let you live *inside* the character. You can tell the story in first-person or third-person close, exploring every doubt and decision. On screen, the point of view is visual. You see what the character sees, but you don't hear their thoughts unless it's spoken. This means the **character's choices and reactions must carry emotional meaning without internal narration**. A stare. A hesitation. A step forward or back. The audience interprets meaning through *performance*. In a novel, the meaning is in the *voice* of the prose.

There's also the question of **audience experience**. A screenplay is meant to be interpreted, performed, and realized by a team. It's collaborative. A novel is complete on the page. It's yours, start to finish. This means that in a screenplay, *suggestion* is powerful. In a novel, *immersion* is key. You need to fill the reader's senses. Let them taste the blood, hear the crunch of bone, feel the ache in the ribs.

So which is better for your martial arts story? That depends on your goals. If you want to write something tight, visual, and performable—go screen. If you want to explore psychology, culture, and inner transformation—go novel. Or do both. A novel can be adapted into a screenplay. A screenplay can be expanded into a novel. Each format strengthens your understanding of pacing, character, and movement.

Ultimately, the heart of the story doesn't change. It's still about someone learning who they are through struggle, through training, through pain. But the way you show that journey—through script or prose—shapes the reader's experience.

One is choreography. One is memory.

Both can strike like a master's blow. You just have to choose the form that lets your story breathe, move, and fight the way it was meant to.

Turning Ancient Wisdom into Fresh Dialogue

Martial arts stories thrive on timeless themes—discipline, balance, inner peace, restraint, humility, and purpose. These ideas have been passed down for generations, echoed in the scrolls of ancient masters, the whispered lessons of wandering sages, and the clipped phrases of grizzled instructors. But when you're writing fresh dialogue for a modern audience, those ancient teachings need to feel *alive*, not dusty. If they sound like fortune cookie clichés or overly formal quotes from a temple wall, you risk losing emotional impact. The challenge is to preserve the depth of the wisdom while speaking with *clarity, humanity, and relevance*. You want the ancient to feel *immediate*.

Start by understanding what ancient wisdom really *is*. At its heart, it's just lived experience filtered through simplicity. These are truths discovered in solitude, in sweat, in silence. "He who hesitates is lost." "Empty your cup." "The softest touch breaks the hardest stone." These lines work because they reflect universal truths in clean, compact form. But in fiction, they can feel tired unless they're rooted in *character*. The master can't just throw out wise sayings like they're handing out fortune slips. The line must come from *knowing*, from having earned it.

So how do you make that kind of dialogue fresh? First, embed it in *emotion and context*. Instead of your master saying, "There is no victory in anger," maybe they say it right after the student lashes out and loses control during a sparring match. They're not reciting a quote—they're speaking *from pain*. Maybe they mutter it, shake their head, walk away. Now the line isn't just wise—it's *felt*. You don't need to explain it. The reader *sees* what it means.

Second, tailor the delivery to the character. A philosophical teacher might speak in full metaphors. A more direct one might just say, "You're not listening to your feet. That's why you keep falling." Same wisdom, different flavor. One way to explore this is to prompt ChatGPT with:

"Write a martial arts master explaining the meaning of patience using different tones—one poetic, one sarcastic, one gentle."

You'll see how delivery shapes impact.

Modernize without diluting. You don't have to translate everything into slang or make it overly casual. But you *can* update the metaphor. Instead of, "Be like water," your character might say, "You keep trying to punch the wave instead of riding it." It's the same truth, just less quoted, more visual. Instead of saying, "Control your spirit," a modern mentor might say, "Your emotions are running your body like a drunk driver. Sit them down."

You can also *invert the cliché*. Maybe the student hears the same line—"Empty your cup"—and responds, "It's already empty. That's the problem." Now the phrase becomes a starting point for deeper dialogue, not a conclusion. That back-and-forth can bring ancient ideas into a new light. The student challenges, and the master reframes. "Then we fill it with something better. Not rage. Not fear. Just presence."

Silence, too, can carry wisdom. Sometimes the best line isn't spoken. A master watches a student fail the same technique again. Instead of correcting them, they walk over, hand them a broom, and walk away. The lesson: control starts with the basics. Humility starts with service. The reader feels the wisdom through *action*, not just speech.

If you want to invent original wisdom rooted in martial philosophy, start with themes: balance, ego, fear, patience, resilience. Then ask ChatGPT something like:

"Give me ten original martial arts proverbs about fear and control."

You'll get raw material—some classic, some new—that you can reshape into dialogue that fits your world and your characters.

Consider *contradictions* too. Martial arts is full of paradoxes. Fight without fighting. Win by yielding. Hit hardest when you don't mean to hurt. Let your characters struggle with these contradictions. Maybe a student repeats a lesson but doesn't understand it—until the moment it *clicks*. That realization moment is where the dialogue lands hardest. Let them say it themselves, finally understanding: "I wasn't losing the fight. I was losing myself."

Your antagonist can twist wisdom too. Maybe they use the same teachings but warp them into justification for violence. "My master taught me to move without thought. So I don't hesitate anymore. Not even when it comes to breaking bones." Now ancient wisdom becomes a battleground, not just background.

And don't forget humor. A master might say something deceptively simple: "You fall like a sack of laundry. Again." That *is* wisdom—wrapped in grumpiness and truth. Not every teaching moment needs to be lofty. Sometimes the student learns through a bruise and a one-liner.

The key to writing fresh dialogue rooted in ancient wisdom is this: *don't preach—evoke*. Let the lesson emerge from the scene, the moment, the mistake. Let your characters speak from experience, not perfection. Even your master is still learning. Even your student sometimes says the wisest line in the room without meaning to.

Because martial arts is more than skill—it's story. And when the words hit like strikes, when the wisdom lingers like a bruise, that's when your dialogue has found its rhythm. That's when old truths feel new again. That's when your reader leans in—not because they want to be taught, but because they want to *feel*.

Symbolism in the Fight: What Every Blow Means

In martial arts fiction, every punch can be more than a strike. Every block can speak louder than words. A fight scene isn't just about who wins or loses—it's a conversation in motion, a physical expression of ideas, emotions, and unresolved conflicts. When written with intent, a fight becomes symbolic. It transforms into a moment where philosophies clash, values are tested, identities shift, and characters are either broken or remade. To make your fight scenes unforgettable, you need to look beyond the choreography and ask yourself: *what does each blow actually mean?*

Start by thinking of each fight as a **narrative device**, not just an action beat. It's a chapter in your character's arc. So before you write the strikes, decide *what the fight represents*. Is it the student proving themselves to a teacher? A warrior confronting their past? A rival trying to validate their own path? Once you know what the fight stands for, every move has weight. A missed strike becomes hesitation. A successful counter becomes growth. A brutal finish might not be a win—it might be a moment of regret, of transformation, of surrender.

Symbolism in combat often comes down to **who the opponent is**. Your antagonist, rival, or training partner should challenge the protagonist not just physically, but philosophically. If your hero believes in mercy, let them face someone who believes mercy is weakness. If your hero has something to prove, let them face someone who doesn't care. Every movement in the fight becomes a metaphor for a belief being tested. A moment of restraint says more than a knockout.

For example, imagine a fight where the hero refuses to land a final blow. That pause, that moment of internal conflict, tells the reader everything. It says, *this fight isn't about dominance. It's about control.* Or maybe the hero uses a technique taught by someone they once hated—suggesting reconciliation, or at least respect. That one move becomes a symbol of growth. And maybe the rival *recognizes* it. They flinch. They react. The fight just turned emotional.

Weapons and techniques can carry symbolism too. A blunt weapon might suggest a desire to subdue, not kill. A quick, evasive style could represent a character who avoids emotional vulnerability. A fighter who never moves backward might be afraid of retreating in life, not just in combat. And when they *finally* step back—when they *choose* to retreat—it's not a weakness. It's a shift in worldview.

Don't overlook the **environment**, either. Fighting in a sacred dojo, an abandoned school, or a collapsing rooftop all adds symbolic pressure. The place can represent history, legacy, or chaos. A duel in the rain might mirror emotional clarity or grief. A sunny open field might become a place of rebirth, or irony, if the violence contradicts the peace of the surroundings. Setting isn't just scenery—it's another layer of meaning.

Timing matters, too. The *first* strike in a fight might carry symbolic importance. It could represent the character's surrender to violence, or their inability to find another solution. A character who never throws the first punch might have a personal code—and breaking that code mid-story tells us everything about how they've changed. Likewise, the *final* blow is your punctuation mark. What kind of period are you putting on this sentence? Is it a knockout that ends with silence? A scream? A nod of respect? The delivery changes the meaning.

You can also use **repetition** for symbolism. A move taught in Chapter 3 that fails in Chapter 8 might finally succeed in Chapter 16—showing growth not just in skill, but in understanding. Maybe a character once struck out of rage. Now, they use the same move with precision and calm. The technique is the same. The meaning is entirely different.

Internal monologue during a fight can guide readers through this. Not so much *explaining* the symbolism, but revealing emotion. Let them feel the doubt before a strike. The memory behind a stance. The pain of using a move that reminds them of someone they've lost. Symbolism doesn't always need to be intellectual. Sometimes it's just *felt*—a physical echo of emotional scars.

Even *loss* in a fight can be symbolic. Maybe the hero loses, but doesn't break. Maybe they win, but lose a piece of themselves. Maybe they stop fighting—and *that* is the act of victory. Winning the battle is never as interesting as winning—or losing—the moment.

To create symbolic fights, ask ChatGPT for layered suggestions like:

"Give me a martial arts fight scene where each movement reflects a character's inner conflict about identity," or

"Describe a final duel where the protagonist uses their rival's technique as a symbol of acceptance."

These kinds of prompts give you motion that already carries emotional meaning—saving time and deepening your scene.

Symbolism isn't about making a fight scene complicated. It's about making it *resonate*. Readers may not remember every move, but they'll remember the moment your protagonist stepped over the line—or chose not to. The moment someone dropped their weapon. Or whispered an apology before the final strike.

So before you write the next punch, ask: what does it *say*? What fear does it mask? What history does it echo? What belief is it challenging?

Because in martial arts fiction, a fist is never just a fist. It's a message. It's a memory. It's a mirror.

And when you write with that level of depth, your fight scenes don't just entertain. They *mean* something. They strike the reader right in the heart—and leave a bruise that tells a story all its own.

The Spiritual Layer of Combat Stories

At first glance, martial arts stories are about movement—about fighting, training, enduring, and overcoming. But look deeper, and you'll find that the greatest of them are never just about fists or feet. They're about *spirit*. Beneath every block and blow is a quiet conversation between the body and the soul. And that's where the spiritual layer of a combat story lives—not in the religion or rituals, but in the inner stillness, the personal reckoning, the search for balance that turns every strike into a question and every silence into an answer.

Spirituality in martial arts fiction doesn't mean your characters need to quote scripture or meditate under waterfalls—though they can. It means they fight with purpose. They train not just to hurt, but to understand. They're seeking something. Not trophies. Not titles. Something intangible. Peace. Redemption. Forgiveness. Identity. The combat becomes a *path*—a way to find clarity through movement, a mirror for the self in chaos.

Think of your protagonist's journey not just as an external arc of skill, but as an inward spiral. Every confrontation isn't just with an enemy—it's with themselves. They face fear, ego, pride, loss, doubt. They struggle to control the fire within. The greatest opponent, in the spiritual combat story, is rarely the rival across the ring. It's the weakness inside. The part of them that wants to give up. The part that fights for the wrong reasons. And when they master that, the external victory becomes meaningful—not just earned, but *enlightened*.

The spiritual layer often reveals itself through restraint. When your character has the opportunity to destroy their opponent but chooses not to—*that* is spirit in action. When they bow after defeat, or fight for someone else, or walk away from a battle that no longer serves them, they're not just showing maturity. They're showing spiritual depth. You can write these moments as quiet beats between punches. A breath. A pause. A look skyward. A flash of memory. The absence of action becomes the story.

Many martial arts traditions speak of *chi*, *ki*, or inner energy—not as magic, but as metaphor. It's the current that flows through controlled breath, focused intent, and unified body-mind action. When your character trains, meditates, or reflects, they're cultivating this presence. You can express this in prose with simplicity. "She exhaled. The fear left with her breath." That's all it takes. The spiritual doesn't need to be lofty—it needs to be *honest*.

Nature is often a spiritual mirror in these stories. The wind, the rain, the stillness of a pond. A warrior looking at a mountain and realizing how small they are. Or standing in the desert, recognizing that power fades, but the earth remains. Use your setting not just for physical context, but for spiritual symbolism. Let your character walk through a storm on the night before the final battle—not just to get wet, but to wash something away. Let the moonlight reflect their fear. Let the sunrise become their redemption.

ChatGPT can help you layer this into your story with prompts like:

"Give me a scene where a martial artist reflects on their purpose before a duel, blending nature and inner clarity,"

or

"Describe a spiritual training sequence where the focus is not on strength, but on letting go."

These moments can act as bridges between fight scenes, giving your story breath and soul.

Spiritual mentors also carry this layer. Not every teacher needs to teach techniques. Some teach presence. A master who refuses to spar but spends time in silence might pass on more than any strike ever could. Maybe they ask questions instead of giving answers. Maybe their greatest lesson is one the student resists until it finally lands—*when they stop seeking victory, they begin to grow*.

And let's not forget the *cost* of violence. A spiritual combat story acknowledges that fighting takes something away, even when it's necessary. Your protagonist might win, but feel empty. They might lose, but find peace. These contradictions are part of the spirit. The final scene doesn't need to be a roar—it can be a whisper. A hand unclenched. A weapon laid down. A student bowing to an opponent who taught them more through pain than words.

The spiritual layer is also about *transcendence*. The moment a character steps beyond fear. When they move not from instinct or anger, but from stillness. You can write this as a flow state in battle—"Time slowed. She didn't think. She didn't react. She simply *was*." That's spirit in motion. The art becomes meditation. The fight becomes liberation.

Ultimately, you don't have to explain any of this to the reader. They'll feel it. In the spaces between your scenes. In the moments where nothing is said, but everything is understood. In the stillness between strikes. That's where the spirit lives.

So when you write your next combat story, ask not just *what happens*, but *what heals*. Not just *who wins*, but *who awakens*. Let your characters bleed, yes—but let them also breathe. Let them walk the path of fists with open hands.

Because at the heart of every great martial arts tale, there's a truth that doesn't need to be spoken. A silence that strikes deeper than any blow. And a spirit that never stops moving, even after the fight ends.

Creating a Legendary Weapon or Fighting Technique

In the world of martial arts fiction, few things ignite the imagination more than a legendary weapon or fighting technique. These iconic elements elevate a story from grounded combat into mythic storytelling. They become symbols—of power, of sacrifice, of legacy. The moment a character draws a blade etched with ancient runes, or strikes with a move whispered about in hushed tones, the audience knows something sacred or dangerous is unfolding. Whether it's a forbidden technique known to break its wielder's body or a blade that chooses its master, these legendary tools don't just look cool—they *mean* something. And that's the key to creating one that truly lasts in your reader's mind.

The first step is to build the **mythology** around it. A legendary weapon or technique must feel like it has a history—something earned, hidden, feared, or misunderstood. Who created it? Why? What happened to the last person who used it? Is it tied to a betrayal, a vow, or a great loss? You don't need to reveal all the details right away. In fact, the mystery is part of its magic. Let the whispers travel ahead of the reality. A student might hear, "No one uses the Thirteen Breath Cut anymore... not since the night the sky caught fire." That one line does more than explain. It *suggests*. It hooks.

When designing a **fighting technique**, start with its *philosophy*. Every great martial arts move should reflect a worldview. If the technique is built on speed, maybe it's about never giving the opponent time to think. If it's about absorbing and redirecting force, maybe it teaches that strength lies in surrender. Maybe the user must empty themselves of emotion to execute it properly—or be overcome by the very energy they try to harness. The deeper the idea behind the move, the more powerful it becomes when it finally appears in the story.

Name it carefully. Names like "The Black Crane's Final Wing," "The Pulse of Stillness," or "The Dragon's Echo" evoke style, motion, and tone. You want a name that feels like it carries *weight*—as if simply saying it is enough to stir tension. Ask ChatGPT to help brainstorm by prompting:

"Give me ten names for forbidden martial arts techniques rooted in emotional restraint or sacrifice."

Then choose the one that resonates with your story's emotional core.

You can describe the technique itself in detail—or keep it poetic. Sometimes it's better to describe the *effect* than the step-by-step motion. "His body vanished in a blink. A heartbeat later, the enemy dropped to their knees, blade still sheathed." The mystery enhances the moment. And if you do want to describe the physical execution, let it unfold slowly. Build the tension. Let readers know that *this* is the move everyone feared, everyone trained for, but only one person ever mastered.

Now let's talk about **legendary weapons**. Like techniques, they need more than flash. They need a *soul*. Why does this weapon matter? Was it forged by a forgotten master? Created from a piece of a fallen star? Bound by a spirit that exacts a toll on the wielder? A weapon becomes legendary not just because it's powerful—but because it *represents* something. Maybe the blade can cut through steel, but only when used in defense of another. Maybe a pair of gauntlets grant immense strength—but amplify the user's rage unless they remain emotionally grounded.

Design matters too. Let the physical features tell a story. A staff cracked in the middle but wrapped in golden thread, said to hold the balance of destruction and restoration. A pair of twin daggers, one warm to the touch, the other always cold—passed down through twin siblings who died in battle. A wooden training sword that's never been sharpened, yet defeated masters of steel through sheer control. The look of the weapon should reflect the *ideology* it was built from.

And don't forget the **price**. Every legendary weapon or technique should *cost* something. Maybe using the move drains the body's energy so severely it can only be used once a year. Maybe the weapon resists unworthy hands and harms those who draw it in anger. Maybe the move can only be taught by someone willing to die after passing it on. That weight makes the choice to use it matter—and raises the stakes every time it appears.

Your story should treat these legendary elements with *reverence*. Don't introduce them casually. Build anticipation. Let characters speak of them in rumors, argue about their existence, even fear them. Then, when the moment comes, slow everything down. Time should feel suspended. Let the reader feel the shift in energy. And when the move lands—or the weapon is drawn—it should feel like a moment the entire story has been moving toward.

Want help generating the specifics? Ask ChatGPT for something like:

"Create a legendary martial arts move that reflects inner peace overtaking inner rage, including history and visual description."

Or

"Design a mystical weapon tied to a broken warrior's past that only works when they accept forgiveness."

You'll get rich starting points to develop further into emotional anchors within your story.

Ultimately, what makes a legendary weapon or technique stick isn't just its power—it's the *story* around it. The beliefs it challenges. The legacy it carries. The transformation it demands.

So craft it not as a gimmick, but as a reflection of your character's journey. Because when the technique is more than muscle—and the weapon more than metal—they stop being tools.

They become myth. They become memory. They become *legend*.

Escaping Clichés While Honoring Tradition

Martial arts stories walk a narrow path between time-honored tradition and the ever-present danger of cliché. The noble master, the hot-headed student, the training montage, the final tournament—all familiar, all potentially powerful. But if handled without care, they risk becoming flat, predictable, and uninspired. The challenge is this: how do you respect the traditions that make martial arts storytelling so rich, while creating something that feels fresh, personal, and *true*? The answer lies not in avoiding tradition—but in reinterpreting it through your characters, themes, and emotional honesty.

Let's start with what makes something a cliché in the first place. It's not the concept itself—it's the lack of *specificity*. A master telling a student to "be like water" becomes a cliché if it's just dropped in because it sounds wise. But if your master says it while the student is struggling with inflexibility in their life—emotionally, mentally, physically—and if that lesson is woven into the story through their choices and setbacks, then it's no longer a cliché. It's a moment of *truth*. The line lives because it connects to something deeper than surface wisdom.

The same applies to structure. The tournament arc? It can be thrilling—if the fights reveal emotional stakes. The training montage? Still effective—if each moment shows frustration, resistance, humility, and growth, not just repetition. Don't ditch the tradition. *Humanize* it. Layer it with feeling. Make it yours.

Characters are often the first place where clichés sneak in. The stoic master with a tragic past. The student who's naturally gifted but undisciplined. The smug rival who gets humbled. These aren't bad characters—they're *templates*. What makes them feel real is the detail. Give your master a sense of humor. Give your rival a point. Give your student not just skill but something to *unlearn*. Ask yourself: what *scares* them? What *surprises* them? What do they believe that's wrong? And how will this journey challenge that?

One of the best ways to escape cliché is to **invert expectations**. Let the master fail. Let the student refuse the call to train. Let the rival become an unexpected ally—or let the real rival be self-doubt. Maybe the final fight ends not with a dramatic strike, but with the protagonist stepping away. Not because they're afraid—but because they finally understand they don't need to win. These kinds of moments honor the emotional *truth* of martial arts far more than a predictable ending.

Another powerful technique is to **ground tradition in culture**. A lot of Western martial arts stories borrow surface elements—belts, kiais, bowing—without understanding where they come from. Dig deeper. Explore the philosophies behind the techniques. Why is silence sacred in some dojos? Why do some styles emphasize yielding over striking? Even if you're building a fictional world, draw on real systems of belief, community, and training that reflect martial values: humility, perseverance, self-control, harmony. When these principles drive your plot and characters, the traditions feel authentic—not borrowed.

Use ChatGPT to help refine these layers. Try prompts like:

"How can I subvert the 'wise old master' trope while still keeping their role meaningful?"

or

"Give me ten alternatives to the traditional tournament arc in a martial arts story."

You'll get new ways to shape the story, while still nodding respectfully to the classics.

Dialogue is another area where cliché tends to creep in. Avoid phrases that feel like they came from a bad action movie. Instead, write dialogue that sounds like *your* characters. A master might not say, "There is no try—only do." They might say, "Trying means you're still afraid to commit." Or maybe they say nothing and just gesture to the broken board on the floor. Let their wisdom emerge through interaction, not slogans.

Also, pay attention to **language and tone**. If your story is modern, don't force an ancient voice. If it's historical or fantasy, don't default to faux-mysticism. Find a consistent, grounded tone that fits the world and characters. Real wisdom sounds simple. It's often quiet. Let that simplicity breathe instead of stuffing it with grand speeches.

The key to honoring tradition is to treat it like a living force—not a statue. Let it shape your characters. Let it evolve. Let it be questioned. Maybe your protagonist learns a style that's been untouched for centuries—only to realize it was built for a different world, and they must adapt it or risk losing themselves. That evolution *is* respect. It says: I learned from the past, but I'm not frozen by it.

And let's not forget humor and imperfection. Sometimes martial arts stories get so heavy with discipline and honor that they forget the joy. The awkwardness of learning. The friendships. The sweat and laughter in the back corner of the dojo. These human elements remind readers that behind the traditions are people—flawed, funny, learning people. That's what brings your story to life.

In the end, escaping cliché while honoring tradition is about writing with **intention**. Know where the story comes from. Know what it means. And then shape it to reflect your characters, your world, and your truth. Because tradition isn't the enemy of originality—it's the foundation. It's what lets your story bow to the past, then step forward, ready to fight its own battle.

Respect the roots. Challenge the form. And tell the story *only you* can tell. That's how you escape cliché—not by avoiding the old—but by giving it *new life*.

The Hero's Physical and Emotional Arc

In every martial arts story worth remembering, the hero doesn't just become stronger—they become *someone else.* Not someone entirely different, but someone *truer.* Someone more aware of who they are, what they fear, what they believe, and what they're willing to fight for. That transformation isn't just a matter of learning how to throw a cleaner punch or mastering a secret technique. It's about inner evolution—becoming a person of greater presence, purpose, and self-understanding. The journey from physical progress to emotional awakening is the very heart of the martial arts narrative. Without both arcs working in harmony, your hero's story won't feel complete.

Let's start with the **physical arc.** This is the surface-level progression—where we see the hero train, sweat, stumble, and gradually grow into someone who can take on increasingly dangerous challenges. Early in the story, their movement is clumsy. Their body is rigid. Their reactions are slow or wild. But through training—usually painful, often humiliating—they begin to move with flow. Their stances deepen. Their strikes get sharper. They learn control. Rhythm. Timing. They don't just fight harder. They fight *better.*

But the physical arc should always be tied to something emotional. What's holding them back? Is it fear? Ego? Guilt? Doubt? Physical improvement alone doesn't make a martial arts story powerful. The real power comes when that physical transformation reflects something inside. For example, a character who's afraid of hurting others might struggle with committing to a strike. A character full of rage might hit hard, but waste energy and lose focus. A big moment isn't just landing a punch—it's realizing *why* they missed the ones before it.

The **emotional arc** begins in parallel but often lags behind. Your hero might learn the moves quickly but still lose fights because their mind isn't clear. They're distracted. They're carrying emotional weight. Maybe they're training to impress someone else. Or to prove something. Or to bury something. That's when your story gets depth—because now, every scene becomes a dual battle. The opponent in front of them, and the one inside.

Your hero's emotional arc might take the form of rediscovering their sense of self. Or letting go of something that no longer serves them. Or realizing that what they thought they wanted—revenge, glory, respect—isn't what they needed. Let those realizations come at moments of stillness and motion. Let a failed fight bring reflection. Let a quiet walk home after training carry more emotional weight than the match itself. Martial arts isn't just about what happens *on* the mat—it's about who the person is when they *step off* it.

A strong way to track the emotional arc is through a single fear or belief that shifts over the course of the story. Maybe your hero begins believing that strength means domination. By the end, they believe it means control. Or maybe they believe they're alone—and slowly, through training and pain and unexpected kindness, they find connection. These shifts make the physical victories feel earned.

And don't forget to let the *body tell the story.* You can show emotion through how your character trains. Are they stiff when sad? Reckless when angry? Do they collapse after a moment of mental clarity, not from exhaustion but from release? Even posture can tell a story. Someone walking into the dojo upright and proud might later enter low-shouldered but humble—and more powerful for it.

The moment where both arcs meet is your emotional climax. Maybe it's the final fight. Maybe it's the moment they choose not to fight. Maybe it's when they teach someone else what they've learned. When the body moves from a place of emotional clarity, that's the moment readers *feel* the growth. That's where your story breathes.

You can plan this fusion with ChatGPT by asking:

"Build a martial arts hero's arc that shows parallel physical training and emotional healing after personal trauma."

Or:

"Describe how a character's fear of failure affects their movement in combat and how they overcome it."

The more you connect physical and emotional cues, the more alive your character becomes.

Let training sequences do more than build skill. Let them reveal vulnerability. Let sparring matches turn into therapy sessions in disguise. Let the master's toughest lesson not be about how to fight—but about *why* not to. Let pain mean something. Let effort bring not just progress, but truth.

The end of your story shouldn't feel like the hero has reached perfection. It should feel like they've reached *understanding*. That their body is ready—but more importantly, their *spirit* is aligned. The world hasn't gotten easier. They've just become someone who can meet it with calm eyes and steady breath.

So write the bruises. Write the sweat. But also write the silence between breaths. The tear that comes before the strike. The joy that blooms after a moment of surrender. Because that's where the real fight happens—not on the mat, but inside.

And when your hero finally moves with purpose—not from fear, not from rage, but from balance—that's when your story ends exactly where it should: with strength, with grace, and with a spirit that's earned every step.

Testing Plot Ideas for Power and Clarity

Every martial arts story begins with a spark—a character, a fight, a philosophy, a question. But once that spark is lit, the story needs to burn with a steady flame. That means your plot needs both *power*—something emotionally compelling, dramatic, and resonant—and *clarity*—a structure that guides the reader or viewer clearly through the journey. It's easy to come up with a cool idea for a fight or a unique training sequence, but it's much harder to know if that idea belongs, connects, or truly drives your story forward. That's where testing your plot ideas becomes a vital part of the writing process.

The first step in testing any plot idea is to ask the most basic and important question: **what is this story *really* about?** If you can't answer that in one sentence, your plot might be full of great moments but lacking a core. For example, is your story about overcoming fear? About the cost of revenge? About honoring a broken legacy? Once you know that center, you can test whether each plot point reinforces it—or distracts from it.

Let's say your plot includes a mysterious fighter who appears mid-story and challenges your protagonist. That's a great scene—but ask: *why does this moment matter?* Does the mysterious fighter reflect a part of the hero's inner conflict? Do they force a new decision? Do they change the direction of the journey? If the answer is "not really," then it might be cool—but not powerful. To make it powerful, tie it back to the emotional core.

You should also test your plot for **stakes**. Every martial arts story needs them—not just "Will they win the fight?" but "What does winning cost? What does losing change?" If your plot idea centers around a tournament, ask: *what happens if the hero loses?* Not just externally, but internally. Do they let someone down? Do they break a promise? Do they lose faith in themselves? The more layered the stakes, the more powerful the story.

Clarity comes from structure. You don't need a rigid formula, but you *do* need progression. A solid martial arts plot typically has key turning points: the call to train or fight, the first real failure, the mid-point moment of clarity or betrayal, the emotional low, the comeback, and the final test. Try placing your plot points along this arc and ask: *does the story build? Does the tension rise? Do earlier scenes set up later payoffs?* If not, you might need to reorder, reframe, or simplify.

Use ChatGPT to help with this process. You can try prompts like:

"Here's my martial arts story idea—does this plot have strong stakes and emotional growth?"

Or:

"Does this mid-point fight support the hero's transformation, or is it just a cool action scene?"

You'll get helpful feedback that helps clarify which scenes serve the whole and which need sharpening.

Another test is the **character drive** check. In every major scene, ask: *Is the hero making choices?* Passive protagonists weaken plot power. Your character doesn't have to win every fight, but they should be *deciding* to enter it. If things just keep happening to them, you lose tension. Powerful plots are built on *decisions*, not coincidences. If a new opponent shows up, the hero should *choose* to engage—or *choose* to walk away. That choice reveals character. That choice fuels plot.

You can also look for **echoes** across the plot. A lesson learned in Act I should be tested in Act III. A technique taught at the start should appear again—used properly this time. These repetitions show growth, mastery, and emotional payoff. Ask: *Does the story reflect on itself? Do the early moments matter later?* These echoes give the plot a feeling of wholeness—and that's where clarity lives.

Another useful test is what we can call the **stripped version** test. Take your story and remove all the fights. What's left? If the emotional arc, the character development, and the dramatic stakes still hold up, then you've got a strong foundation. Now the fights become *enhancements*, not crutches. You'll know your plot works not because the action is cool, but because the story *moves*.

Also, test the pacing. Print out your plot in bullet-point form. Look at the spacing between major moments. Are there long stretches without meaningful change? Too many fights back-to-back without emotional consequence? A dip in tension halfway through? These moments are plot signals. Adjust the pacing so each scene flows into the next with intention.

And finally, test your ending. Martial arts stories aren't just about the final fight—they're about the final *shift*. Ask: *what has the hero learned? What have they let go of? What are they still holding onto? What's changed inside them, even if they didn't win?* If your final scene reflects the opening but reveals growth, then your plot has emotional power *and* clarity.

So go ahead and play with bold ideas. Invent lost techniques. Create rival dojos. Build betrayal arcs, stormy final battles, and near-death moments. But always test: *does this serve the story? Does it make the character grow? Does it make the reader feel something true?*

Because when your plot is both powerful *and* clear, the story doesn't just entertain. It *moves*. It flows like a fight. It hits like a lesson. And it stays with the reader long after the final bow.

Using Flashbacks for Tragedy and Motivation

Flashbacks in a martial arts story are more than just memory—they are echoes of pain, moments of clarity, and windows into the reason a character fights at all. When used with purpose, a flashback becomes the emotional engine behind the action. It's the bruise that never healed, the loss that shapes every move, the moment that birthed a vow. Especially in stories centered on discipline, training, and personal growth, flashbacks let us glimpse the raw wound beneath the strength. They give the reader not just *what* the character is doing—but *why*.

But there's a danger in using flashbacks carelessly. If dropped in without context or used purely for exposition, they can disrupt pacing, confuse timelines, or pull the reader out of the narrative. The goal is not to interrupt the story—it's to *deepen* it. The trick is knowing *when* to use a flashback, *why* to use it, and *how* to frame it so that it lands like a well-placed strike: fast, clean, and meaningful.

Start by deciding what emotional truth the flashback will reveal. Maybe your protagonist is cold and distant—then we learn through a flashback that they lost someone because they hesitated in a fight. Suddenly, that coldness is armor. That stoic training routine is grief in disguise. Now every present-day decision they make carries hidden weight. Or maybe the character pushes too hard, never rests, never forgives weakness. A flashback shows a father who punished failure with silence and shame. Now we see the drive, but also the damage. The flashback doesn't just explain—it *transforms* how we understand the character.

The most powerful flashbacks are often **emotional counterpoints** to present-day action. A character wins a fight—flashback to the moment they were beaten to the ground by a sibling who later died. A character hesitates before a killing blow—flashback to the day they accidentally hurt someone they loved. These moments *intercut* between what's happening now and what shaped it, creating a rhythm that binds past and present like call and response.

Let the flashback arise *organically*. A smell. A sound. A training movement. A specific technique. These sensory cues can trigger memory, just like in real life. If your character is performing a kata, and suddenly they remember being corrected by their now-deceased teacher, the transition feels natural. It's not a clunky narrative jump—it's a flow of memory. Ask ChatGPT for help with this using prompts like:

"Give me a flashback triggered by a martial arts stance that reminds a fighter of a lost loved one."

Also, keep flashbacks **focused and intentional**. Don't let them drift or become mini-stories. A tight flashback can be just a paragraph—a line of dialogue, an image, a sensation. "He stepped into the stance. His right foot forward, the same way his brother had stood that last day. The day he didn't come back." That's enough. The reader fills in the rest with emotion. You don't always need the full scene. Sometimes the absence—the suggestion—is more powerful.

When you *do* write a full flashback scene, make sure it serves the plot and the emotional arc. Does it change the way the character behaves afterward? Does it shift the reader's sympathy? Does it reveal the *motivation* behind the mask? If not, consider saving it or trimming it. Flashbacks are too potent to waste—they should be emotional turning points, not just backstory delivery.

You can also use **mirrored structure** to make flashbacks more meaningful. If your character hesitated to protect someone in the past and paid the price, show them facing the same choice again. Will they freeze, or act? The flashback builds tension because the audience *knows* what happened before. Now they're holding their breath, waiting to see if the character can finally break the cycle.

Flashbacks are especially strong when dealing with **trauma or tragedy**. Martial arts stories often feature heroes who have lost something—a sibling, a parent, a master, a version of themselves. These flashbacks can reveal the *depth* of that loss. But don't over-explain. Let the imagery speak. "The dojo was quiet. Rain on the roof. The mat still stained from the last lesson. He hadn't been back since." That's all you need sometimes. Let the quiet moments hold the loudest echoes.

The best flashbacks don't just show *what happened*. They show how it *still hurts*. The scar under the bandage. The hesitation before a familiar move. The breath your character takes before speaking a name they haven't said in years. These moments are where readers lean in—not for spectacle, but for truth.

Use ChatGPT to help structure them. Try:

"Create a flashback for a martial arts protagonist haunted by a fight that ended a friendship,"

or

"Write a memory that explains why a hero refuses to use a particular technique."

Then shape those responses into emotional beats that connect directly to your present-day plot.

And remember: flashbacks don't always need to be sad. They can show joy that's been lost. A training day full of laughter. A student looking up to their master. A lesson that once made no sense, now remembered with clarity. These moments soften the story and give the pain more contrast.

Ultimately, a flashback should feel like a strike from the past—sudden, precise, and impossible to ignore. When done right, it leaves the character changed, the reader moved, and the story deepened.

Because in a martial arts tale, it's never just the fight that defines the hero—it's the *memory* of why they learned to fight in the first place.

Making Your Hero Earn Every Victory

In martial arts storytelling, the moment the hero wins—whether in a brutal final duel, a high-stakes tournament, or a quiet decision to walk away from the fight—is a moment that should *resonate*. But for it to truly hit the heart, that victory must be *earned*. Not just by training harder or fighting better, but through personal struggle, emotional growth, painful failure, and transformation. When a hero is handed victory without challenge, it feels hollow. When they earn it—sweat, scars, soul and all—it becomes unforgettable.

The first step to making a victory feel earned is to start your hero in a place of *true weakness*. Not just physical inexperience, but emotional immaturity, fear, ego, or confusion. Maybe they're impulsive, driven by revenge, or seeking validation. They might think that winning a fight will fix everything. Let that be their belief early on—and then let the story challenge that belief until it breaks. A hero who starts strong and stays strong is boring. A hero who is broken and rebuilds themselves—through discipline, humility, and introspection—makes every victory feel like a *revelation*.

Next, you need to give your hero **meaningful losses**. Failure is where growth lives. Let them lose a fight early on. Let them lash out, hesitate, choke. Let them walk away ashamed. And don't make these failures just mechanical—they should hit emotionally. Maybe they get outclassed by a rival who trained harder. Maybe they abandon their principles and win dirty—and feel worse for it. Or maybe they lose someone they care about because they weren't ready. These setbacks become the foundation for real transformation.

To make victory feel earned, every challenge your hero faces must *cost* something. Time, relationships, innocence, certainty. Maybe they miss family milestones because they're obsessed with training. Maybe their health begins to fray. Maybe they have to walk away from people who don't understand the path they've chosen. These sacrifices build a quiet gravity behind their journey. They show the reader that every gain comes with a price.

The training scenes should reflect not just physical exertion, but *internal change*. Don't just show them getting faster or stronger. Show them becoming more patient. More self-aware. More focused. Maybe they train alone in the cold, repeating a movement for hours not to master a technique—but to confront a memory they've been avoiding. Let those moments of stillness carry just as much weight as a fight scene. Growth isn't always loud.

Make your hero's **choices** matter. They shouldn't win because they stumbled into luck or because someone else bailed them out. They should make tough calls—ethical, emotional, tactical. Maybe they choose to fight someone they know they'll lose to, because it's the right thing to do. Maybe they choose to fight *without* the forbidden technique they've been dying to master. Maybe they choose to save a rival rather than finish the match. These decisions define the *kind* of hero they become—and make the final victory feel like it belongs to someone who's earned it through *who they are*, not just what they can do.

Victory doesn't need to mean domination. In fact, it often lands harder when it's *quiet*. When the hero wins not by striking harder, but by standing still. By showing mercy. By letting go. Maybe they lose the fight, but gain self-respect. Maybe they don't win the title, but they reclaim their soul. The best victories often aren't about beating someone else—they're about *overcoming the person they used to be*.

Use ChatGPT to test this arc. Try prompts like:

"Describe a martial arts hero's internal change over three fights, showing how each loss shapes their final victory."

Or:

"Create a scenario where the hero wins without landing a single blow, but the victory still feels earned."

Let your story build tension around what winning *means*. Early on, maybe it means proving something. Midway, it means surviving. In the end, it means understanding. Every fight, every step, should pull the hero toward a clearer version of themselves. A version that doesn't just *deserve* victory—but *understands it*.

Supporting characters can also reflect how far the hero has come. A rival who once mocked them now nods in respect. A mentor who said they weren't ready now watches silently, proud but wordless. A friend who saw them fail now sees them rise. These reactions become the chorus around the moment of victory.

Finally, take your time with the *moment after* the win. Don't rush to credits or conclusions. Let the hero breathe. Let the reader breathe. A quiet scene where the hero wraps their knuckles, stares at an old photo, or simply walks home under streetlights, is often more powerful than cheers and applause. It's the emotional exhale that confirms this journey was worth it.

Because when a hero earns every victory—physically, emotionally, spiritually—the story leaves a mark. It doesn't just thrill. It *transforms*. And that's the kind of story that stays with the reader long after the final bow.

Story Beats That Lead to the Ultimate Confrontation

Every great martial arts story builds toward a moment—the ultimate confrontation. It's the clash where everything comes to a head: skill, philosophy, pain, and growth. But this moment can't just appear out of nowhere. It needs to be *earned*, built step by step through story beats that raise the stakes, test the hero, deepen the conflict, and prepare the audience emotionally for what's about to go down. You don't just want a good fight. You want a fight that *means something*—where every punch echoes with purpose and every choice feels like the final piece in a puzzle that's been slowly coming together since page one.

Let's look at how to design the journey that leads there.

It all begins with the **inciting incident**—the moment that sets the story in motion. This could be a humiliation, a personal loss, a challenge, a call to train, or an injustice witnessed. Whatever it is, it must knock the hero out of their comfort zone and point them toward a fight they are not yet ready for. Maybe a rival humiliates them. Maybe a dojo is burned. Maybe a loved one is harmed. The key is: this moment creates a deep personal reason to grow. The confrontation begins *here*, even if the fists don't fly until much later.

Next comes the **refusal or misdirection**. The hero doesn't jump straight into training or revenge. They hesitate. They deny. Or they chase the wrong goal—maybe they think beating people up will restore their confidence, or they obsess over a forbidden technique. This beat shows they're not ready emotionally. It gives room for the real journey to unfold. Their idea of what the final fight means is *wrong*. They must be shown—through trial, through loss, through teaching—that victory is not what they think it is.

Then comes the **training and transformation** phase. This is where they begin to change, both physically and internally. They start learning skills, but more importantly, they begin confronting the things holding them back: ego, anger, fear, doubt. It's not just about growing stronger. It's about becoming *someone new*. Maybe they fail again. Maybe they lose a sparring match that should've been easy. Maybe a mentor says they aren't ready. This is the beat where the protagonist's body is sharpening—but their spirit is still uncertain.

You'll then want to introduce a **rising threat or challenge** that directly relates to the ultimate confrontation. The rival becomes more dangerous. The stakes go up. Someone close to the protagonist gets hurt. A promise is made. An opportunity is lost. This beat is important because it shifts the story from training and preparation into personal commitment. The hero *chooses* the path now. They're no longer running from the fight. They're walking toward it.

Somewhere near the middle of the story, there should be a **mirror moment**—a scene where the hero sees themselves reflected, usually through someone else. Maybe they meet a fighter who used to be like them and ended up broken. Maybe they see their rival act with a kind of discipline they haven't mastered yet. This is the wake-up call. It reminds them that the final confrontation isn't just about defeating someone else—it's about not being defeated by who they used to be.

You'll then want the **emotional low point**. This is the beat where everything breaks. The hero loses a fight they should've won. Or they betray a principle. Or someone they care about walks away. Maybe their training collapses under pressure. Maybe they return to the place where it all began and feel like nothing has changed. This moment is painful—but necessary. It clears the ego. It forces reflection. And it makes what comes next *earned*.

After this, give your protagonist a moment of **clarity or insight**. They revisit a lesson from earlier and *finally understand it*. They reconcile with their master. Or with themselves. They go back to basics. They simplify. They breathe. This isn't a moment of triumph. It's a moment of stillness—of knowing. And from this, they rise again, not as someone chasing strength or vengeance—but as someone who *knows who they are*.

This leads us to the **final preparation beat**. Think of it like the calm before the storm. The hero wraps their hands. Faces their fears. Says goodbye to someone. Looks at their reflection. There is no more noise. No more uncertainty. This is the moment the reader knows: *it's time*. Let this beat breathe. Let it hum with tension.

And then—*the ultimate confrontation*. This is not just a fight. It's the final test of everything the protagonist has learned. It should be layered. Physical on the surface. Emotional beneath. Philosophical at the core. The opponent shouldn't just challenge them with fists—but with *ideas*. This is the moment where technique, training, pain, and identity all come together.

Let the fight evolve. Start with brutality. Shift to strategy. End with emotion. Let your hero make a choice—not just to win, but to become something greater. Maybe they use a move they swore they never would. Maybe they fight without anger for the first time. Maybe they refuse to finish the fight when they could. The point is: they are no longer the person they were when this journey began.

And once it ends, let the moment settle. The crowd silent. The breath held. The dust falling. Let it land.

Use ChatGPT to help test and sharpen these beats. Try prompts like:

"Outline a martial arts story that builds to a confrontation with a rival who represents the hero's former self."

or

"Write five emotional turning points that lead a martial artist from revenge to self-realization."

In the end, the ultimate confrontation isn't great because it's epic. It's great because it's *inevitable*. Every beat that came before pointed to this. Every lesson, every failure, every bruise. This is where the hero proves not just their skill—but their *truth*.

That's how you build a martial arts story that hits harder than any punch—because it strikes at the heart.

How ChatGPT Can Help You Build a Tournament Bracket

Tournaments are a staple of martial arts storytelling. They bring structure, tension, escalating conflict, and a natural path to a climactic showdown. Whether your story features an underground fight ring, a sacred festival combat event, or an international martial arts competition, the tournament gives you a ready-made framework to test your protagonist against a range of opponents. But designing a tournament that feels balanced, unpredictable, and emotionally satisfying can be time-consuming. That's where ChatGPT steps in—not as a shortcut, but as your creative collaborator.

To start building your tournament bracket, first decide how many fighters you want. A simple 8-fighter bracket is manageable. A 16-fighter setup adds complexity. Go higher, and you'll need a system to manage pacing and character development. Once you've picked the size, ask ChatGPT:

"Create a 16-fighter single-elimination martial arts tournament bracket, with unique names, fighting styles, and brief backstories for each fighter."

You'll instantly have a full roster of characters, each with flavor, identity, and potential plot hooks.

Want to add cultural depth or variety? Try a prompt like:

"Design a martial arts tournament with fighters from different nations, each with a fighting style tied to their homeland's philosophy."

Now your bracket has both spectacle and theme. It's not just about winning—it's about worldview clashes, cultural expression, and ideological conflict. Your hero isn't just facing physical tests—they're confronting ideas, values, and legacies.

Once your bracket is in place, you can use ChatGPT to plan out the **match order** and outcomes. Prompt:

"Show the round-by-round winners in this tournament and how each fight pushes the protagonist to grow emotionally or physically."

This turns your tournament from a checklist of battles into a story structure, with character development embedded in every round. Maybe the first match forces your hero to face someone they admire. The second pits them against someone who fights dirty. The third makes them face someone with a personal connection to their past. With each round, the stakes and the meaning of each fight increase.

Want unexpected twists? Ask:

"Suggest five ways to surprise the reader during a martial arts tournament without breaking the internal logic of the story."

You might get ideas like a shocking upset, a fighter withdrawing for personal reasons, or a rigged match that throws everything into question. These surprises don't just keep things interesting—they create new dramatic arcs.

You can also ask ChatGPT to help choreograph individual matches. Say:

"Describe a quarterfinal match between a defensive grappler and a reckless striker, with tension and emotional stakes."

This gives you cinematic action with narrative tension already baked in. You're not just getting "who hits whom"—you're getting *why it matters*.

Another powerful tool? **Using ChatGPT to simulate character arcs through the bracket.** Maybe your rival enters the other side of the tournament. Ask:

"Build a subplot around the hero's rival who fights his way to the final from the opposite side of the bracket, with a redemptive arc."

Now the final match means something beyond just skill—it's about past wrongs, parallel journeys, and the emotional resolution readers crave.

Don't forget the **non-combat elements**. You can prompt:

"What traditions, rituals, or rules might make this tournament culturally unique?"

Or:

"Describe the atmosphere of a legendary martial arts tournament, including the crowd, announcers, and ceremonial openings."

This adds richness to your world. Maybe fighters bow before each round. Maybe there's a silent tribute before the finals to honor fallen masters. Maybe the arena itself has a mythic history. These touches make your tournament feel lived-in and legendary.

ChatGPT can also help you troubleshoot pacing. Try:

"How do I pace a martial arts tournament in a novel without making it feel repetitive?"

You'll get guidance on balancing training sequences, off-stage match results, character subplots, and emotional fallout between matches—so your tournament breathes, rather than dragging.

And of course, let ChatGPT help you map the visual side. Ask it to:

"Create a text-based visual layout of a tournament bracket showing who fights who in each round."

It'll give you a clear structure to follow as you write or revise.

Whether your story is a classic underdog tale, a redemption arc, or a revenge saga wrapped inside a tournament, ChatGPT can help you design a bracket full of tension, transformation, and storytelling precision.

Because in the end, a great martial arts tournament isn't just about climbing to the top. It's about *what gets revealed* on the way up—and who your hero becomes by the time they get there. With the right matchups, momentum, and meaning behind every round, you'll build a tournament that feels less like a structure and more like destiny.

Writing the Fall and Rise of a Martial Arts Champion

One of the most emotionally compelling arcs in martial arts storytelling is the fall and rise of a champion. It's the narrative that hits hard, not because of the fights themselves, but because of the *loss of identity* that follows a fall—and the painful, personal journey of reclaiming strength, meaning, and purpose. A champion who starts on top and loses everything is already gripping. But it's the slow, humble rise back to power—not just physical, but spiritual—that transforms a story from entertaining to unforgettable.

To write this kind of story, you need to begin with the **high point**. The reader must believe in your champion. They must see what makes them extraordinary—not just their skill, but their presence. Their confidence. The way others look at them. Maybe they've never lost a fight. Maybe they won a brutal tournament, took down an unbeatable rival, or are considered a living legend. Start with an iconic moment. A big win. A crowd chanting. An award in hand. Let the glory feel real.

But beneath that victory, seed the *flaw*. The crack in the armor. Maybe they're too confident. Maybe they're fighting for the wrong reasons. Maybe they're already burning out and can't admit it. The fall shouldn't come from nowhere—it should feel like a delayed inevitability. You can foreshadow it with a quiet conversation, a moment of hesitation, or a missed detail that others ignore. This builds emotional suspense.

Then comes the **fall**—and it should *hurt*. Bad. Maybe they lose a fight they were supposed to dominate. Maybe they're publicly humiliated. Maybe they're betrayed. Or maybe they're injured—physically broken in a way that puts their entire future in question. This isn't just a defeat. It's the destruction of who they thought they were. They don't just lose the fight—they lose the *identity* of "champion." That's the real gut-punch.

What follows is **disillusionment**. The silence after the fall. The loss of followers, of friends, of purpose. Maybe they can't even look at the dojo. Maybe they throw away their belt. Maybe they drink. Hide. Lash out. Withdraw. The important thing here is that the story *pauses*. Let the stillness settle in. Don't rush the comeback. This is where the soul of the arc lives. In the questions. In the doubt. In the question of *who am I if I'm not the best?*

Eventually, something must break that silence. A **catalyst**. It could be external—a new threat, a student in need, a mentor reaching out. Or internal—a moment of clarity, a memory, a quiet realization that strength without purpose means nothing. This spark is *not* the rise. It's the first flicker of movement.

Then comes the **rebuild**—slow, awkward, painful. They return to training, but it's not the same. The body doesn't move like it used to. Their instincts are rusty. They doubt every move. They get beat by someone they would've laughed at before. This part of the story should feel like the inverse of the champion's prime. It's humbling. It's necessary. Let the champion *learn again*. This is where they become a student of themselves, of their flaws, of the path they forgot.

During this phase, let them confront what broke them. Maybe it wasn't just the loss—it was the reason they fought. Maybe they realize they were fighting for applause. Or revenge. Or pride. The rise only truly begins when they find a *new reason to fight*. One rooted in love, duty, peace, or redemption. This moment must feel *earned*. Not dramatic. Not cinematic. Quiet. Clear. "I'm not fighting to win anymore. I'm fighting to be whole."

Now you can begin the **return to form**—but don't make it a full circle. Let them fight differently. Wiser. More grounded. Less flashy. More intentional. Maybe they even give up a signature move because it no longer fits who they are. Maybe they train with someone they once mocked. Maybe they find peace in their losses and no longer fear them.

When they step back into the arena—or into the final confrontation—it should be not as the same person they were before, but someone transformed. Not just a fighter. A human being who knows what fighting *means*. Their rise is not about reclaiming a title—it's about reclaiming themselves.

Let the **final confrontation** reflect that growth. Maybe they fight a version of their younger self—a hungry rival who fights recklessly. Maybe they face the one who beat them. Or maybe it's an old friend turned antagonist. This fight should be as much about *control* and *restraint* as it is about power. The crowd may cheer, but the champion no longer fights for them.

Use ChatGPT to help layer this transformation with prompts like:

"Give me a martial arts training scene where a former champion struggles with self-doubt and begins to rediscover purpose."

Or:

"Describe a climactic fight where the hero chooses clarity and restraint over revenge."

And when the story ends, don't focus on the victory. Focus on the *stillness* that follows. The moment the hero breathes out. Smiles. Bows. Maybe they walk away from the spotlight. Maybe they pass the torch. The rise doesn't have to be loud. It just has to be true.

Because the most powerful stories aren't about those who never fall. They're about those who fall *hard*—and rise with grace, humility, and a spirit wiser than the one that first touched the mat. That's how you write a champion who doesn't just win again, but becomes *worthy* of being remembered.

Exploring Inner Demons through Outer Conflict

Martial arts stories have always walked the line between the physical and the psychological. While the outer conflict—punches, kicks, tournaments, duels—grabs attention and raises adrenaline, the *inner demons* of the character are what give these battles weight. The most unforgettable fights aren't just against opponents. They're against the fear of failure, the shame of the past, the desire for vengeance, or the loss of identity. And when you craft your story so that every external fight is a metaphor for an internal struggle, you transform your narrative into something truly profound.

To explore inner demons through outer conflict, you start by clearly defining the **psychological core** of your protagonist. What do they carry that they've never faced? What haunts them? Is it guilt over a failed promise? A betrayal they never recovered from? A fear that they're not good enough, or worse—that they're *too much like the person they hate*? This core truth doesn't need to be shouted. It just needs to shape how they move, how they speak, and how they fight.

The next step is to construct external conflicts that don't just challenge them *physically*, but *symbolically*. Your hero isn't just facing opponents who hit harder—they're facing opponents who *mirror* their inner world. A fighter who mocks their failures. A rival who shares their fighting style but wields it with cruelty. A student who's becoming everything the hero was before they fell. These fights become reflections—living, breathing reminders of what they haven't resolved inside themselves.

Think of it this way: **every outer conflict is a doorway to inner confrontation**. When your hero clashes with a powerful adversary, ask: *What does this person represent emotionally or philosophically?* A quiet, precise fighter might reflect a hero's need for control. A berserker brawler could force them to confront their own buried rage. A fighter who refuses to fight might test the hero's understanding of mercy. In each case, the fight isn't just about dominance—it's about *revelation*.

You can build this metaphorical structure by asking ChatGPT for support:

"Create a martial arts antagonist who represents the hero's fear of becoming ruthless,"

or

"Design a rival fighter whose philosophy of strength challenges the hero's belief in compassion."

By pairing each external conflict with a piece of internal conflict, you ensure that every confrontation pushes the hero *deeper into themselves*, not just forward in plot.

Let the emotional toll show during fights. A character who hesitates mid-strike because a move reminds them of a violent past. A fighter who's too eager to win and overcommits, revealing a desperate need for validation. A moment of silence after a victory that feels more like defeat. These layers bring out the spiritual and psychological aspects of combat, and they make readers feel like they're witnessing something more than technique—they're witnessing *truth* under pressure.

Use flashbacks, internal monologue, or even symbolic choreography to highlight this. Maybe your protagonist uses a move they swore never to use again. Maybe they drop into a stance their master used—and realize how much they miss them. These small beats inside a larger action sequence create enormous emotional payoff. The audience doesn't just watch the fight. They *understand* the cost of it.

At the midpoint of your story, include a fight your hero *wins* physically but *loses* emotionally. Let them beat the opponent but feel hollow. Let them hear applause but feel ashamed. This is often the clearest moment where inner demons are at their loudest. And it sets up the transformation that will lead to a more *authentic victory* later.

Eventually, the final confrontation must be *less about winning*, and more about *facing the self.* Maybe the hero refuses to fight altogether. Or maybe they fight, but with new understanding. They see their opponent not as a threat, but as a reflection. Maybe the final move isn't the one that defeats the opponent—but the one that shows *mercy*, or *restraint*, or *forgiveness*. That's how inner demons are resolved—not by crushing them, but by *recognizing* and *owning* them.

You can experiment with moments like these using ChatGPT:

"Write a scene where a martial artist realizes their opponent fights with the same anger they've been trying to let go of."

or

"Describe a moment in battle where the protagonist hesitates and sees a reflection of their younger self in the rival's movements."

These moments don't just elevate the drama—they create a story that resonates beyond the mat or arena. They invite the reader to reflect on *their own* inner conflicts. And they remind us that martial arts is not just about defeating others—but about mastering ourselves.

In the end, the most powerful battles in your story will not be the flashiest. They'll be the ones where the reader realizes the hero isn't fighting to prove something—they're fighting to *become* something. And when that happens, every punch lands not just on flesh, but on fear. Every block protects not just the body, but the soul. And every victory feels like redemption—not just for the hero, but for the *person they were* when the story began.

Showing Growth through Fighting Style Evolution

In a martial arts story, a character's fighting style is more than a method of attack—it's a mirror of who they are. The way they move, strike, block, hesitate, and recover reflects not just their training, but their mindset, their emotional state, their past, and their purpose. That's why one of the most effective ways to show character growth is to let their fighting style evolve as they do. It's a visual, visceral way to track transformation—and when done right, it tells the reader everything they need to know without saying a word.

To start, define your character's **initial style** based on who they are at the beginning of the story. Are they aggressive and reckless? Their fighting might be wild, fast, and untamed—full of brute strength and little control. Are they anxious and unsure? Maybe they flinch easily, stay on defense, or hesitate before every move. Are they cocky and overconfident? Perhaps their strikes are flashy, unnecessarily risky, all flair with little depth. Early in the story, your character should fight the way they *think* they need to—but not the way they *should*.

Let that initial style *fail them*. Maybe it works against weak opponents, but breaks down under pressure. Maybe it gets them hurt. Maybe it causes collateral damage. Whatever happens, this failure should be a turning point—an emotional beat that pushes the character to reflect, to change, or to relearn. This is the first step in evolution: *confronting limitation*.

Use this moment to transition into a new phase of their journey. Perhaps they go back to basics. Perhaps they seek a new teacher. Perhaps they fight someone who shows them what real mastery looks like—and it's nothing like what they're doing. This begins the process of *shedding ego and embracing discipline*.

During the middle of your story, their style should begin to shift—subtly at first. Maybe they stop relying on brute force and begin to use timing and positioning. Maybe they start to observe before reacting. Maybe they lose fights but *learn* from each one, adjusting their rhythm and approach. These changes don't have to be spelled out. Let readers see it in the way they dodge a blow they would've taken earlier. In how they stop attacking just to prove something. In how they move with purpose instead of pride.

You can ask ChatGPT to help with this by prompting:

"Show how a martial artist's fighting style evolves from aggressive and chaotic to calm and precise over three key fights."

Or:

"Describe a training scene where the character begins to adopt a new style that better reflects their inner transformation."

Think of this evolution in terms of **philosophy**. Every style reflects a belief. If your character once believed that strength was about domination, and later learns that strength is about control, their style must reflect that shift. Instead of breaking every defense with force, they begin to redirect, conserve, and choose their moments. Their body becomes quieter. Their movements, more thoughtful. Their power, less visible—but far more dangerous.

You can also use physicality and technique to show emotional growth. A character who once fought with clenched fists and bared teeth now fights with relaxed shoulders and calm breath. A fighter who used to go in swinging now waits, watches, and finishes fights with minimal effort. They're not just more skilled. They're more *centered*. Their fighting has become an extension of who they've become.

You can mirror this shift through specific techniques. Maybe they had a signature move that defined them—something big, fast, and hard-hitting. Let them abandon it when they realize it no longer serves them. Or let them *transform* it. What was once a move used in rage is now delivered with quiet intent. That move, once reckless, becomes *refined.* It doesn't just land harder. It *means* more.

This kind of transformation also shines in contrast to rivals. Let the opponent remain the same—wild, rigid, cruel—and show how the hero, once similar, now moves differently. Let the rival flail while the protagonist flows. The difference in style becomes the difference in character. The reader sees, clearly, who has grown and who has not.

And if your story includes a final fight, let this be the moment where the new style *fully emerges.* Not as a trick or sudden surprise, but as the natural result of everything the hero has endured. They fight as someone who *knows who they are.* Someone who no longer fights to win, but to protect, to stand for something, or to bring peace.

The evolution of style can also reflect healing. Maybe the hero had a shoulder injury from a traumatic fight. As they heal emotionally, they begin to trust that shoulder again—shifting their stance, opening up new moves they had shut off before. This ties body and spirit together in a powerful way.

If you want to design these arcs in detail, try this:

"Create a progression of three fighting styles for a martial arts character who starts off angry and reckless, then becomes patient and balanced, and finally transcends violence altogether."

Because when your character's fighting style evolves with their story, the action becomes more than spectacle—it becomes a language. It speaks of pain, progress, purpose. It shows us who the character *was*, who they *are*, and who they are still becoming.

And in martial arts storytelling, that's the real victory—not in how many fights they win, but in *how* they fight by the end. With clarity. With discipline. With meaning. With truth.

Setting the Scene: Dojos, Mountains, Underground Rings

In martial arts fiction, the setting isn't just where the story happens—it's where the soul of your story *lives*. The right environment doesn't just hold your characters—it challenges them, shapes them, reflects their inner struggles, and adds texture to every fight and moment of stillness. Whether it's a sacred mountain, a run-down inner-city dojo, or a brutal underground fight ring, your settings should breathe with mood, energy, and meaning. They're not background—they're characters in their own right.

Let's start with the **dojo**. This is often the emotional heart of a martial arts story—the place where the student trains, breaks, learns, and rebuilds. A well-written dojo scene feels like entering a world governed by ritual and legacy. The scent of sweat and wood polish, the sound of fists hitting pads and the silence that follows a bow—these are details that set the tone. A dojo can feel ancient, spiritual, and quiet—or modern, practical, and intense. You decide what kind of story it tells just by how it looks and sounds.

But the dojo isn't just physical. It carries the weight of its teacher's philosophy. A strict, traditional master may run a space lined with calligraphy scrolls, tatami mats, and incense. A progressive coach might teach in a converted garage with mirrors, steel beams, and Bluetooth speakers blasting music during drills. The way students behave, speak, and move in the dojo can communicate everything about the kind of world they're living in.

Now contrast that with the **mountains**—the classic training ground of solitude and spiritual growth. This setting removes distractions, comforts, and outside noise. It's where the protagonist confronts themselves. Training in a mountain setting doesn't just test the body—it tests the *will*. The cold, the altitude, the silence—these elements become part of the story. A lone student practicing forms at dawn, breath fogging in the chill air, is more than a visual—it's a metaphor for focus and rebirth.

Mountain settings also connect the character to nature. They can symbolize clarity, elevation, and the climb toward something greater. Use this space for your hero's emotional turning points. Maybe it's where they break down after a failure. Maybe it's where they begin to see the connection between mind, body, and spirit. The terrain itself can become part of the training. Balancing on rocks. Climbing cliffs. Practicing in the snow. The elements become part of the challenge—and part of the transformation.

Then we have the opposite: the **underground fight ring**—a space filled with shadows, noise, blood, and desperation. This setting is gritty, raw, and chaotic. Here, the rules are unclear or nonexistent. Fighters don't bow. They don't respect. They survive. An underground ring is perfect for showing what happens when martial arts loses its soul. When fighting becomes currency instead of discipline. The lighting is harsh. The crowd is drunk. The floor is sticky. And in the center of all of it is your protagonist, surrounded by noise but entirely alone.

The underground ring is a crucible. It's where characters are pushed to their limits, tempted to become something darker. Maybe your hero enters it out of necessity, or anger, or as a test. Maybe they win, but feel hollow. Or maybe they lose, and it changes them. This setting reveals the underbelly of the martial world—the place where ego, money, and pain blur the line between fight and survival.

You can use ChatGPT to help you create rich environments by asking:

"Describe a traditional Japanese dojo run by a master who values silence and self-control."

Or

"Give me sensory details for an underground fight club held in a former subway station."

The responses will give you atmosphere, objects, sounds, and moods to work with.

And don't forget other unique locations. A rooftop under the rain for a secret duel. A bamboo forest where the wind interferes with every move. A rooftop dojo above a busy city, full of modern distractions. A prison yard where martial arts is learned out of survival. The best fight scenes happen in places that *amplify the stakes*. Where every corner, every sound, and every texture matters.

Also, consider **emotional layering**. Maybe your character returns to the dojo where they once trained—but it's abandoned now, quiet and dust-covered. Maybe they revisit the mountain where they failed years ago. Maybe they step into a ring not as a fighter, but to stop a fight. Let the setting carry memory. Let it speak.

Settings don't just support your scenes. They *shape* them. They provide resistance, symbolism, energy, and silence. The setting your characters fight in should test them as much as the opponent in front of them.

Because in martial arts storytelling, where the fight happens matters just as much as how it unfolds. A well-chosen setting turns a strike into a statement, a pause into reflection, a win into a transformation. And when you bring those spaces to life, your story doesn't just move—it *lives and breathes* with every step, stance, and breath your characters take.

Themes of Revenge, Redemption, and Respect

Martial arts stories are more than just physical confrontations—they are emotional, philosophical, and deeply personal journeys. At their core, they often wrestle with three timeless themes: revenge, redemption, and respect. These aren't just narrative devices; they're the emotional engines that power every fight, every loss, and every hard-earned victory. Each one offers a unique path for your characters to walk, and when woven together, they elevate your story into something that resonates far beyond the ring or the dojo floor.

Let's begin with **revenge**, the most explosive of the three. This is the spark that lights countless martial arts tales. A sibling killed in a street fight. A master betrayed. A brutal loss suffered at the hands of a merciless rival. Revenge gives a character drive—but it's a dangerous kind of fuel. It burns hot, fast, and unpredictably. A character consumed by revenge fights not to grow or protect, but to hurt. That impulse can carry them far, but it often leads to destruction—of others or of self.

What makes revenge compelling is watching how it *changes* a character. At first, it might sharpen their focus, give them the discipline they lacked. But the closer they get to their goal, the more they must confront what that goal will cost them. Maybe they start becoming like the person they hate. Maybe they win—but find that it doesn't heal anything. Or maybe they lose, and realize that revenge was never the answer. The best revenge arcs are the ones that *don't resolve through violence*, but through reflection. Through transformation. When you show a character turning away from revenge, choosing peace or mercy instead, you elevate the story from one of pain to one of *growth*.

Then there's **redemption**. This theme speaks to characters who have done wrong—or believe they have—and are seeking a way to make it right. Redemption arcs are deeply human. They begin with shame, regret, guilt. Maybe your protagonist used to fight for money and hurt people who didn't deserve it. Maybe they abandoned a student or let pride ruin something sacred. Redemption is not about undoing the past. It's about owning it—and choosing to be better.

What makes redemption powerful is how hard it is. Your character doesn't just get forgiven. They must struggle. They must face the people they hurt. They must change, not through one act of bravery, but through *consistent discipline*. In martial arts fiction, this often means training again, humbling oneself before a former rival, or protecting someone they once would have ignored. Redemption isn't clean. It's full of setbacks. But when a character earns it, the emotional payoff is immense.

You can even layer these themes together. A former villain now fights for redemption—but the person they wronged is still on a path of revenge. Now your story isn't just about fists—it's about conflicting journeys of healing and vengeance. These kinds of emotional collisions are what give a fight scene its *real weight*. When the audience understands what's at stake inside the characters, every punch lands harder.

Then there's **respect**—a quieter theme, but no less essential. Respect is the heartbeat of martial arts culture. It's found in the bow before a spar, the nod after a loss, the silence in the dojo. Respect is what separates martial arts from brawling. It's what turns violence into discipline, what turns opponents into teachers. In storytelling, respect shows character growth. A fighter who once mocked others may learn to honor even their enemies. A student who once fought for glory may come to respect the journey itself more than the victory.

Respect often evolves through the story. At first, your protagonist might crave recognition, mistake fear for respect. But true respect is earned, not demanded. It grows in the spaces between fights—how the character treats others, how they carry themselves after a loss, how they react to defeat or criticism. A character's greatest moment might not be a victory at all, but how they handle the moment right *after* they've been beaten.

These three themes can also **intersect**. Imagine a character who seeks revenge, only to find redemption through an opponent who shows them respect. Or a once-proud champion who disrespected their students, now humbled and fighting for the respect of the very people they failed. Or a master who has lived in shame, redeeming themselves by preventing their student from taking a violent path of revenge. These emotional dynamics are where your story becomes more than action—it becomes *human*.

You can use ChatGPT to help layer these ideas. Try prompts like:

"Give me a redemption arc for a disgraced martial arts champion who once fought for ego,"

or

"Create a story where a martial artist must choose between revenge and earning the respect of their enemy."

These kinds of narratives give you more than plot—they give you a *moral journey*.

When you write with these themes in mind, every fight becomes more than physical. It becomes spiritual. Philosophical. Emotional. The story no longer hinges on who wins—it hinges on *why they're fighting*. And when your reader sees that, they connect not just to the story—but to something deeper in themselves.

Because revenge may light the fuse. But it's redemption and respect that carry the heart of the martial arts story across the finish line—with dignity, with wisdom, and with power.

Gender, Identity, and Power in Martial Arts Stories

Martial arts stories offer one of the richest canvases for exploring themes of gender, identity, and power—often because these stories are already rooted in transformation, control of the body, and the journey toward self-mastery. Whether your narrative takes place in a traditional dojo, a futuristic tournament, or a gritty street circuit, your characters are constantly grappling with questions of who they are, how they're perceived, and what it means to be powerful in a world shaped by social expectations and personal truth. When you weave gender and identity into this framework with care and intention, you create a story that hits far deeper than any flying kick ever could.

Let's start with **gender**—not just as a checkbox, but as an experiential reality. Martial arts fiction has a long history of showcasing male protagonists, often with a focus on strength, dominance, and legacy. But gendered assumptions about who gets to be powerful—or how power must be expressed—are exactly the kinds of walls that great storytelling can break down. A female fighter may face external challenges: being underestimated, being excluded, or being pressured to prove she belongs. But more interesting than the external conflict is the *internal dialogue*. What does it mean to wield violence in a world that told her to be small, quiet, or accommodating?

You don't need to make your story about gender to let gender dynamics influence it. A woman who chooses a fluid, elusive fighting style may be seen as weak—until she dominates through technique and timing. A trans character may struggle not just with physical training, but with reconciling body and identity, using martial arts as a form of reclamation. Nonbinary characters may find deep meaning in fighting styles that reject rigid structure in favor of adaptive flow. These experiences can be gently embedded in how a character moves, trains, and grows—no speeches necessary.

Identity goes beyond gender, of course. A character's sense of self may be tied to heritage, family expectations, past trauma, or even the need to *become someone else*. Martial arts stories are fertile ground for these questions. Is the protagonist fighting to uphold a legacy, or to escape it? Do they wear a name they chose—or one they were given? The journey of a fighter is so often the journey of a person learning to define power for themselves. And that power doesn't have to look like muscle and rage. It can be *precision. Presence. Peace.*

One way to explore this is through contrasting fighters. Maybe your protagonist faces someone who represents an old-school, hyper-masculine ideal—brute strength, domination, no emotion. Their opponent scoffs at their style, their identity, their expression. But over the course of the story, your protagonist doesn't beat that figure by out-muscling them. They win by being *authentically themselves*. That's the narrative reversal that makes martial arts stories sing: the idea that the truest strength comes from *alignment*—of body, mind, and identity.

You can reflect these ideas through **style and form**. A character who starts by mimicking someone else's style—perhaps one taught to them as the "right" way—might eventually develop a new technique that blends elements from different traditions, expressing who they are in every motion. This kind of personalized martial arts development becomes a metaphor for identity itself: tested, redefined, and finally embodied.

You might also explore the **emotional cost** of not being allowed to fight as oneself. Perhaps your character was told to suppress part of their personality. To move a certain way. To fight with restraint when they're furious, or to be aggressive when they seek peace. These internal contradictions can lead to a "broken" form—sloppy, un-centered, ineffective. The turning point in your story could be when they *stop performing* and start fighting with intention that comes from within.

If you're writing a story about someone discovering or affirming their identity through martial arts, let the physical act of movement, breath, and repetition become a kind of grounding ritual. Let the repetition of kata or forms become a source of comfort. Let the breaking of form be a symbolic rebellion. Let the body, often politicized, judged, or controlled, become a source of *autonomy*. A place of *truth*.

ChatGPT can help you explore these themes by prompting:

"Write a martial arts training scene where a nonbinary student struggles to conform to a rigid tradition but begins developing a new fighting style that feels true to their identity."

Or

"Create a rival who challenges the protagonist's self-expression and forces a philosophical battle over what real strength looks like."

Also consider using *relationships* to explore gender and power. A mentor may hold outdated views that get challenged. A friend or rival may initially misunderstand the protagonist's identity—but later become an unexpected ally. Power in martial arts stories isn't just about physical ability—it's about who holds authority, who gets listened to, who gets to lead, and who gets to be seen. Let your characters fight those battles, too.

Remember that respect—the quiet bow, the nod after a match, the shared breath before the first strike—transcends identity. And yet, the *path to being respected* can look very different for characters whose identities fall outside traditional norms. That struggle, when told honestly and with empathy, creates stories that are not only powerful, but necessary.

Because in the end, martial arts isn't just about technique—it's about *truth through movement*. It's about discovering who you are when the noise fades, the fight begins, and you have nothing left to hide. And when your story lets a character find power in their own form, their own rhythm, their own voice—you've done more than write a fight story.

You've written a journey of becoming.

Mixing Martial Arts with Other Genres

Martial arts fiction is incredibly versatile. Its foundation—discipline, combat, philosophy, and transformation—lends itself beautifully to a wide range of other genres. When you mix martial arts with science fiction, fantasy, horror, romance, mystery, or even comedy, you unlock new layers of storytelling. The kicks and kata are still there, but they're now part of something bigger: a new world, a different tone, or a thematic twist that deepens the experience. The goal is not to dilute martial arts, but to *expand* its narrative power by combining it with genre elements that create contrast, conflict, and surprise.

Let's start with **martial arts and science fiction**. Think cybernetic fighters, neural-enhanced reflexes, and underground fight tournaments on Martian outposts. The philosophical aspect of martial arts—control, clarity, restraint—becomes especially powerful when contrasted with high-tech augmentation or dystopian systems that dehumanize people. A warrior who rejects enhancements to rely on their own honed instincts? That's compelling. A master who teaches forgotten techniques in a world obsessed with machines? Even more so. The setting can influence the fighting style itself. Imagine martial arts adapted to zero-gravity environments or digital arenas where movement becomes code. It's action with conceptual flair.

Now consider **martial arts and fantasy**. This is where martial traditions take on mythic weight. Your fighters might wield enchanted weapons, draw on elemental powers, or train under immortal masters hidden in mountain temples. The martial arts styles themselves can be entirely invented, each one tied to a sacred animal, a forgotten god, or a lost empire. But even in the most fantastical world, the emotional core remains the same: a character searching for balance, discipline, or redemption. The key is grounding the magic in martial philosophy. Don't just make spells flashy—make them feel like the natural extension of a body, a breath, a belief.

Martial arts and horror? Absolutely. In this mix, martial discipline becomes a survival mechanism. A protagonist trained in control and focus must now face supernatural threats that can't be blocked or dodged. The dojo becomes a sanctuary—or a trap. Imagine a cursed kata that summons spirits when performed. Or a fighter battling inner demons while trapped in a haunted temple. The horror genre amplifies the psychological side of martial arts. Every opponent is not just a monster, but a reflection of fear, guilt, or trauma. The quiet discipline of martial arts becomes a weapon against chaos—until it starts to crack.

Martial arts works surprisingly well with **romance**, too. The intimacy of sparring, the tension of teacher-student dynamics, the vulnerability that comes from training together—it all sets the stage for emotional connection. Two rivals who fall for each other through mutual respect. A former champion finding new purpose—and love—in a student. Or a couple whose relationship is tested by competition, ambition, or the burden of legacy. Fighting side by side or against one another becomes a metaphor for trust, fear, and emotional distance. Done right, the romance adds stakes to the fights, and the fights add fire to the romance.

Then there's **mystery and detective fiction**. Picture a martial artist investigating a crime in the martial world—maybe a murdered master, a rigged tournament, or a missing scroll containing a deadly technique. Now, every opponent isn't just a suspect, but a puzzle. Martial discipline helps the protagonist stay focused while navigating deception and danger. The mystery genre pairs perfectly with martial arts because both are about observation, patience, and timing. The final confrontation is not just about finding the truth—but surviving long enough to reveal it.

You can even blend martial arts with **comedy**—and not just slapstick. Imagine a washed-up fighter teaching a group of misfit kids. Or a rival dojo feud that spirals out of control with ridiculous challenges. Or a protagonist who's really bad at fighting but keeps getting into increasingly absurd martial situations. The comedy works best when it pokes fun at genre tropes—the overly serious master, the dramatic training montages, the mysterious scrolls—and still leaves room for heart. Let the comedy emerge from characters trying earnestly to do something they're not good at yet. That's where the laughs and the love come from.

To develop these genre-blending stories, ChatGPT can help with prompts like:

"Write a story summary where a martial artist in a cyberpunk city must stop a rogue AI using ancient techniques."

Or:

"Describe a martial arts romance set in a fantasy world where rival clans fall in love during a sacred tournament."

Or even:

"Give me a horror-mystery plot where martial arts students begin disappearing from a remote training temple."

When blending genres, always let martial arts remain *central*. The fights, the training, the discipline—they ground the story. The other genre layers add tone, stakes, and theme. You're not covering martial arts with glitter—you're *infusing* it with color, flavor, and depth.

Ask yourself: what happens when martial tradition collides with magic? When control meets chaos? When fists fly in a haunted alley or on the surface of the moon? That's where stories become unforgettable.

Because martial arts isn't a genre—it's a *language*. And when you let it speak across genres, it tells stories you've never seen before but somehow *feel* like they've been waiting for you all along.

How to Design a Training Arc That's Not Boring

Training arcs are the backbone of martial arts stories. They're where the hero grows stronger, both physically and emotionally. They're where philosophies are tested, limits are pushed, and identity is forged. But here's the challenge—training arcs can easily fall into a predictable rhythm: montage, improvement, minor setback, more training, sudden breakthrough. If readers know exactly how it's going to go, it quickly becomes background noise. So how do you make a training arc that's not just informative, but *unskippable*? You make it personal, dynamic, and full of story—not just sweat.

First, understand that training isn't about showing improvement. It's about *revealing character*. At the beginning of the arc, your protagonist may think they're here to learn punches and kicks, but the reader should feel the deeper layers. What are they trying to prove? Who are they trying to impress—or forget? What are they terrified of failing at? Every repetition, every misstep, every moment of exhaustion should *reveal* something. If your character's emotions are shifting, if they're breaking down and rebuilding in real time, then the training *means* something.

Start the arc with a problem that isn't purely physical. Maybe your character is too reactive. Maybe they can't focus. Maybe they think they're better than they are. Then let the training *confront that flaw*. A good training arc doesn't just push the body—it pushes the ego, the fear, the emotional baggage that's in the way of progress. A punch isn't just a punch. It's control over anger. A stance isn't just balance—it's presence. Make that connection clear and the scene goes from functional to unforgettable.

Change the rhythm. Don't structure the arc like a checklist of drills and skill upgrades. Break it up. Let there be awkward failures. Unusual assignments. Emotional pauses. Maybe the master says nothing for days, forcing the student to learn through frustration. Maybe the lesson is disguised—carrying buckets of water uphill turns out to be a test of core strength and mental focus. Maybe the student thinks they're making no progress—until one day, their body responds on instinct. These *moments of realization* are your gold.

Use setting to keep things fresh. If every scene is in the same dojo, it starts to blend together. Shift locations. Have them train in rain. On cliffs. In the dark. Each setting challenges them in a new way and keeps the reader's senses engaged. A forest teaches awareness. A city street teaches adaptation. A mountain path teaches endurance. And every place leaves its mark on your character—not just physically, but emotionally.

Add *conflict within the training*. A rival in the same class. A teacher who's emotionally unavailable. A fellow student who keeps failing and brings everyone down. Or internal conflict—your protagonist struggling with why they're even doing this. Maybe they miss someone. Maybe they're afraid they'll never be good enough. Let those moments *interrupt* the training. Because real growth doesn't happen in straight lines—it happens through struggle, questioning, and reframing.

You can also show the passage of time *creatively*. Don't just say, "weeks passed." Show the changes in how the character reacts to things. Maybe they used to grunt in frustration every time they failed. Now they breathe, reset, and try again. That's growth. Maybe their bruises don't bother them anymore. Maybe their morning routine becomes meditative. The small behavioral shifts are far more compelling than big power-ups.

Let ChatGPT help you map this out. Try prompts like:

"Create a training arc where a martial arts student learns discipline through silent observation instead of physical drills."

Or:

"Write a training sequence where a student realizes their problem isn't physical weakness but emotional fear of failure."

These give you direction for arcs that mean something *more* than just becoming stronger.

Use symbolism to tie it all together. Maybe a broken wooden post represents their old limitations. Maybe a torn sash becomes a reminder of humility. When the training arc includes objects, traditions, or rituals that evolve along with the student, the growth becomes *tangible*. They're not just leveling up—they're shedding something old and stepping into something new.

A great training arc ends not when the student is ready—but when they realize what they were preparing for all along. Maybe they thought it was about revenge, but it's actually about healing. Maybe they wanted to fight someone else—but really, they needed to face themselves.

And that final training moment? Make it quiet. Let it be a breath. A bow. A moment where the student executes a move without effort, without thought—where the growth is clear not because someone says it, but because we *see it*. They've changed. We believe it.

That's how you write a training arc that's never boring. You stop thinking of it as the prep before the story—and make it the *heart* of the story. Because that's where the real battle always begins—not in the ring, but in the mind. And every drop of sweat, every scar, every quiet moment on the mat... that's where the soul of your martial arts tale comes to life.

Making Every Enemy Teach the Hero Something

In the best martial arts stories, the hero doesn't just defeat their enemies—they *learn* from them. Each opponent, each challenger, each obstacle is more than just someone to overcome. They're mirrors, tests, and sometimes reluctant mentors. Whether it's a brutal rival, a cunning trickster, or a quiet assassin, every enemy your hero faces should offer a lesson. Some lessons are painful. Some are unexpected. But all of them shape the hero's path, forcing them to grow not just stronger—but wiser.

To make this happen in your story, you need to think of enemies not as obstacles, but as *reflections*. Each one should challenge a different aspect of your hero's character. If your protagonist is reckless, give them a disciplined enemy who punishes every mistake. If they fight with anger, introduce a calm opponent who absorbs that fury and waits. The fight then becomes more than physical—it becomes *philosophical*. A clash of values, beliefs, and mindsets.

Take a moment to map out your hero's internal flaws and fears. Then design enemies who *embody* the opposite. A brutal opponent can test their restraint. A manipulative enemy can test their clarity. A desperate fighter might remind them of who they used to be—or who they might become if they lose their way. The point is to make each enemy *mean something*. When they fall, the hero should not just be closer to the goal—they should be further along their *journey*.

One powerful approach is to assign each enemy a *lesson theme*. For example:

- **The First Opponent:** Teaches humility. The hero loses. Badly. They thought they were ready—they weren't. This lesson opens the door to real training.
- **The Technical Opponent:** Shows them that raw power isn't enough. Precision and patience matter. This opponent frustrates them, but forces them to refine their technique.
- **The Moral Opponent:** Isn't evil—just driven by a different code. Maybe they believe in justice through fear, or honor through isolation. Their presence forces the hero to question their own motivations.
- **The Mirror Opponent:** Shares the hero's background or fighting style, but has taken a darker path. This fight becomes personal—a warning of what the hero could become if they lose their way.
- **The Unexpected Opponent:** Smaller, weaker, underestimated. And yet, this fighter nearly wins. They teach the hero not to judge by appearances—and not to rely solely on what's visible.
- **The Final Opponent:** Represents everything the hero has yet to master. The fight is not just physical—it's spiritual. Winning requires letting go of ego, fear, or pain.

Each enemy should leave *a mark*—not always a scar, but a *change*. Maybe the hero picks up a movement, a mindset, a saying. Maybe they begin to respect someone they used to hate. Maybe they walk away from a fight not proud—but thoughtful.

You can use ChatGPT to help shape this dynamic. Try:

"Create five martial arts opponents who each force the hero to grow in a different emotional or philosophical way."

or

"Describe a fight where the hero learns more from losing than they would have from winning."

The lesson doesn't always have to be noble. Sometimes an enemy teaches the hero what *not* to do. Maybe the rival who wins at any cost shows the hero how empty that kind of victory feels. Maybe a cruel fighter wins a match and still walks away unsatisfied, revealing that strength without purpose is hollow. The fight ends—but the reflection lingers.

Also consider how your hero responds after each encounter. A win can inflate the ego—or challenge it. A loss can shatter pride—or plant the seed of resilience. The way they digest each lesson shows us who they are becoming. You don't need a speech after every battle. Sometimes it's just a glance. A breath. A changed rhythm in the next fight.

And don't forget: not all enemies have to stay enemies. Some can become allies, rivals, teachers, or even friends. The enemy who taught the hardest lesson might be the one who respects the hero the most. And when that respect is returned, your story takes on an emotional depth that few things can match.

Because in martial arts, the path isn't about crushing everyone in your way—it's about learning from every encounter. Victory becomes transformation. Conflict becomes clarity.

When every enemy teaches your hero something, the story stops being about fighting *against* others—and becomes a journey toward fighting *for* something greater. That's how you turn enemies into milestones. And a simple fight scene into a chapter of true growth.

How to End the Story with a Meaningful Fight

A martial arts story without a final fight is like a journey without a destination. But the *kind* of fight that ends your story determines whether your reader walks away cheering—or quietly reflecting. It's not just about choreography or stakes. The final fight should carry the full weight of your protagonist's journey, emotionally and thematically. It's not about whether they win or lose—it's about what the fight *means*.

The first step to crafting a meaningful ending is to ensure the final confrontation isn't just the *biggest* fight—it's the *most personal*. It should echo everything the protagonist has learned and everything they still fear. Whether they're facing a rival, a former friend, a powerful enemy, or even a student who's surpassed them, this fight must feel inevitable. Not just because it's the climax, but because it's the final test of who your character has become.

That means your final opponent isn't just another obstacle. They're a reflection of the protagonist's journey. Maybe they embody the path your hero *almost* took—the one fueled by vengeance, pride, or unchecked power. Or maybe they represent an old version of the hero: someone who still clings to the belief that strength is all that matters. In that case, the final fight isn't about proving superiority. It's about proving transformation.

You want the fight to feel earned. That starts with silence. The moment before the fight begins—no music, no dialogue, just breath and presence—is one of the most powerful beats in any martial arts story. Let the audience *feel* the anticipation. Let the character check in with themselves. Are they calm? Afraid? Grounded? This is the moment that says, "I've come a long way from who I was."

Now build the fight in stages. Start with emotion. Let old grudges, pain, or doubt drive the first few exchanges. Maybe your protagonist is off balance. Maybe they're fighting out of fear or habit. But then something shifts. A remembered lesson. A breath. A moment of clarity. From here, the choreography becomes *expression*. Every move should reflect a choice. Maybe they don't take the easy win. Maybe they don't respond to taunts. Maybe they fight defensively, using control over aggression.

One powerful approach is to let the protagonist *use something they once failed at*. A technique they couldn't master. A principle they rejected. A philosophy they once mocked. This shows growth not just in skill—but in spirit. The victory, if it comes, feels like closure—not just a triumph of fists, but of character.

You can make the fight even more meaningful by reversing expectations. Maybe your protagonist doesn't win. Maybe they surrender. Maybe they show mercy. If they started the story thinking power was everything, ending it by walking away from a fight can be the most powerful move they make. The reader will feel the weight of that decision—because the journey made it matter.

Or maybe they *do* win—but it's not satisfying. Maybe they see their opponent's pain. Maybe they realize that winning didn't fix the thing they thought it would. In that moment, the reader understands: this fight wasn't about beating someone else. It was about becoming someone better.

Let ChatGPT help if you want to map out such scenes. Ask:

"Write a final martial arts fight scene where the hero's growth is shown through restraint, not victory."

Or

"Describe a fight where the protagonist uses their opponent's own philosophy against them."

Even the *environment* of the final fight matters. Maybe it's the same place where the story began—a burned-down dojo, a sacred hilltop, a public arena now quiet. This adds emotional resonance. It says: the setting hasn't changed, but the fighter has. The world looks the same—but the hero sees it differently now.

And finally, think about the *after*. Don't rush it. Let the hero breathe. Let them bow. Let them return to their master or student or rival and *be seen*. A simple exchange—a nod, a tear, a handshake—can be louder than victory shouts. And if no one's watching, even better. The final fight ends with a moment of quiet self-acceptance. That's the mark of a martial artist—not that they won, but that they found stillness in the storm.

So don't end your story with just action. End it with *meaning*. Let every strike, block, and decision echo the journey your hero has walked. That way, the final fight doesn't just end the story—it completes it.

Because the most powerful fights aren't about proving who's stronger. They're about showing who's finally *whole*.

Writing the Final Line like a Final Blow

The last line of your martial arts story is the final movement in your narrative kata. It's the final breath after the final strike. The punctuation mark that lands not just on the page—but in the reader's chest. You want it to *linger*, to feel sharp, or serene, or inevitable—whatever truth your story was building toward. Like a final blow in combat, it should feel earned, timed perfectly, and delivered with purpose.

To write that kind of line, you first need to understand what the story was *really* about. Not just in plot—but in transformation. Did your protagonist learn to let go of anger? To accept themselves? To understand that strength is not domination, but control? Your last line should crystallize that growth. It's not a summary. It's a *reveal*. A clean cut that says: this is who they are now.

The best final lines are often *simple*. They don't explain. They *land*. A few well-chosen words that carry the weight of everything that came before. Maybe your hero bows quietly. Maybe they whisper a lesson their master once said. Maybe they smile—not because they won, but because they finally understand. That's what you want: *not closure, but clarity*.

Consider these types of endings, and how each one might deliver a final emotional strike:

1. The Echo Line – This mirrors something said earlier in the story, now with new meaning.

First line of the story: "I'll never bow to anyone."

Last line of the story: "He bowed, and for the first time, it felt like strength."

2. The Silent Ending – Sometimes no grand statement is needed. Just an image.

He tightened his belt, stepped onto the mat, and took a breath.

3. The Philosophical Finish – A truth quietly spoken, earned through sweat and pain.

"Some fights end when the fists stop. The real ones end when the heart does."

4. The Turn of Peace – The opposite of what the reader expected.

He dropped his stance. "I don't need to win anymore."

5. The Quiet Walk Away – The story doesn't end with a fight. It ends with what the fight changed.

He walked home, barefoot, bruised, and finally free.

If your story is fast-paced and intense, your last line can be abrupt—a hit that snaps the reader out of the ring. If your story is thoughtful and reflective, your last line should settle in like the last breath of a meditation. Either way, you want the reader to *feel* it.

You can experiment by giving ChatGPT your story's ending and asking:

"Give me five final lines that reflect the emotional transformation of a martial arts protagonist who let go of vengeance."

Then adjust the tone, shorten, stretch, or reshape until it lands with the right weight.

Don't be afraid to rewrite the last line ten, twenty, thirty times. You're not just wrapping up a plot. You're delivering the final emotional strike of the story—the last beat that the reader takes with them. It's not about cleverness. It's about *truth*. And truth always hits harder when it's delivered with restraint.

So when you write that final line, make it count. Make it honest. Make it feel like the final blow of a master—not because it's loud, but because it *lands clean*. Then walk off the page, like your protagonist would—no need to say more. The story is over. The lesson is complete. The spirit has spoken.

How ChatGPT Keeps You Moving When You Stall

Every writer hits a wall. In martial arts, it's the plateau where the moves stop flowing and the muscles ache with every repetition. In storytelling, it's that frustrating moment when the words dry up, your plot feels uncertain, and your characters just stand there, waiting for you to figure out what happens next. But just like a good teacher or training partner pushes you forward when you're stuck, ChatGPT can step in as your creative sparring partner—helping you keep writing, keep thinking, and most importantly, *keep moving*.

When you stall, the first thing ChatGPT can offer is **momentum**. You don't always need a perfect solution—you just need *motion*. That's where prompting becomes your lifeline. Can't figure out how to write a training montage? Ask:

"Give me a training scene where the hero breaks down before they break through."

Now you've got a jumping-off point. You don't have to use it word for word—but it kicks the dust off your wheels.

Sometimes the stall comes from not knowing what happens next. You've got your protagonist mid-arc, mid-fight, mid-realization—but you can't feel your way forward. That's when you ask ChatGPT to help *bridge the gap*. Try:

"What might happen after a martial arts student fails their first major test but still believes they're meant for more?"

You'll get emotional beats, plot turns, and even small visual details that might light a fire under your fingers.

Other times, you know what needs to happen, but the *words won't come*. The scene feels flat. You keep rewriting the same sentence. That's your cue to shift tactics. Let ChatGPT write it in another tone:

"Rewrite this fight scene with more internal emotion and less detailed choreography."

Or

"Write this dialogue scene as if both characters are hiding something from each other."

Changing the angle helps you see the story from a new perspective, and suddenly, things begin to click.

You can also use ChatGPT to keep **emotion flowing** when your writing starts feeling mechanical. If you're stuck in plot but disconnected from feeling, prompt:

"What is my character *really* afraid of in this moment?"

Or

"Show me a small memory that would resurface right before this fight."

Now the character moves with emotional intention—and you write with *meaning* again.

Sometimes you stall because you're simply tired of thinking. You've made too many decisions, stared at the screen too long, and the creative engine is sputtering. That's when ChatGPT becomes your **idea generator**. You can ask it to brainstorm ten alternate outcomes for a scene, five different training obstacles, or new character quirks to spice up a chapter. You don't even need to love any of them. What matters is that they give you *something* to respond to. Writers don't need perfect ideas to get back in motion—they just need *any idea* to wrestle with.

And let's not forget the *tone stall*—when you're writing a story that feels too serious, too slow, or too repetitive. ChatGPT can help you infuse a scene with a new flavor. Ask:

"Add a little humor to this intense training scene without making it silly."

Or

"Turn this quiet character moment into a small but emotional victory."

Tone tweaks can rejuvenate a scene and remind you why you love writing this story in the first place.

One of the most powerful uses of ChatGPT is as a **reflective partner**. If you don't know what's wrong, say that:

"I'm stuck. Here's what I've written so far. Why isn't this working?"

Now you're not talking to a blank page—you're in dialogue. ChatGPT will spot structure issues, pacing lags, flat emotion, or unclear motivations. You're still the author, still in charge—but now you've got a coach in your corner, helping you reframe the problem.

You can also use ChatGPT to review what you've written when self-doubt starts creeping in. Ask it to summarize your last chapter, highlight your protagonist's growth so far, or tell you how a reader might be feeling at this point in the story. This helps you step outside your own head and see the work from a broader angle—often enough to move forward with confidence.

Because at the end of the day, writer's block isn't a wall. It's a fog. And ChatGPT is a flashlight. It doesn't erase the work or walk the path for you—but it shines enough light to let you take one more step. Then another. And another.

So when the story stalls, don't panic. Don't quit. Just shift your weight, take a breath, and tag ChatGPT in. It's here to spar, to prompt, to provoke, and to remind you that the story's not done.

You're still in the fight.

Editing a Martial Arts Story for Flow and Force

Once the first draft is finished—fights written, arcs closed, character journeys complete—it's time to edit. But editing a martial arts story isn't just about fixing grammar or trimming exposition. It's about sharpening rhythm, tightening impact, and ensuring every movement, moment, and line lands with *flow and force*. You want your story to move like your characters do—graceful, powerful, precise. So how do you take your raw draft and tune it to hit harder and read smoother? You edit with the same principles your fighters train by: clarity, intention, and presence.

Let's start with **flow**. This is the reader's experience of moving through the story—scene by scene, sentence by sentence. A martial arts narrative must feel like momentum. The pacing should match the rhythm of a fight: building tension, quickening with urgency, and allowing breath during quiet reflection. The best stories don't just carry the reader—they *pull* them.

Begin by reading your story aloud. Does it *breathe*, or does it stumble? Do sentences trip over themselves or carry the energy forward? In action scenes, short sentences often punch harder. In introspective moments, longer lines can stretch like a meditative exhale. Make your structure echo the emotional tone. If a fight is chaotic, let the rhythm stutter and surge. If a moment is calm, let it linger.

Next, look for **drag**. These are the spots where the story slows down—not to create tension or emotion, but because something's clogging the pipeline. Too much exposition before a fight. Too many internal thoughts when the reader's expecting motion. Too much description in the middle of action. If a fight begins and you spend a paragraph detailing the arena, it kills the energy. Move the description *before* the action starts—or let it unfold during the fight itself, through what the fighter *notices* in real-time.

Now let's talk about **force**. This is the *impact* of the story—what hits the reader emotionally, visually, and viscerally. Force comes from clarity and weight. Is your character's goal in each scene clear? Is the conflict sharp? Are the stakes felt—not just told?

In fight scenes, you want every strike to *matter*. Cut out generic punches and kicks unless they're part of a rhythm. Instead of "He kicked him in the chest," try "His heel cracked against the sternum like a hammer on stone." Now it's not just contact—it's *force*. But don't overwrite. Let the important hits land with vivid detail, and let the others move quickly. It's all about balance.

Dialogue is another key area. Martial arts stories often involve themes of discipline, power, legacy, and restraint. That means characters speak with intent. Go through every line of dialogue and ask: *Is this true to the character? Does it serve the moment? Is it too much?* Especially in mentor-student scenes, it's easy to get preachy. Pare back. A quiet look or a short proverb can hit harder than a speech.

Use ChatGPT as an editing assistant. Feed it a scene and prompt:

"Tighten this scene for pacing and clarity without losing emotion."

or

"Make this fight scene more dynamic and visceral while keeping it readable."

Let it generate a revision, then cherry-pick the strongest parts and blend them with your own voice. You're not giving up control—you're sparring with the page.

Another editing layer to look at is **character consistency**. Is your protagonist's fighting style evolving throughout the story? Do they move, think, and speak differently by the end? Is their final fight a reflection of everything they've learned—not just technically, but emotionally? Re-read early and late scenes side by side. The difference should be clear. If it's not, edit to emphasize growth—not through exposition, but through behavior and movement.

Then there's **emotional flow**. Each major scene should leave an emotional footprint. After a fight, your character should be changed—even slightly. Are they shaken, empowered, ashamed, clear-eyed? Don't rush to the next plot point. Let the emotion land. Let the reader *feel* it. If a character walks away from a battle unchanged, it better be intentional—and even that says something.

Pay attention to **transitions**. If your story jumps too quickly from one scene to another, the momentum stutters. Add one or two lines that guide the reader's eye: a gesture, a sensory detail, a beat of silence. These act like footwork between strikes—making sure the next movement lands clean.

And lastly, polish your final page like a fighter preparing for a final bout. Read it again and again. That last scene, last moment, last line—that's your knockout. Make sure it doesn't just resolve the plot, but completes the *emotional arc*. Make sure the reader closes the book and feels like they've just been on a journey through pain, breath, sweat, stillness, and victory—not because your hero won, but because they *changed*.

Editing is not clean-up. It's the second kata. The time when you take the raw movements and shape them into mastery. Let ChatGPT be your training partner. Let your instincts lead. Trust your pacing. Feel the story's heartbeat.

Because a martial arts story isn't just about what happens—it's about how it *feels* to move through it. When your edits find that flow and force, the reader won't just read your story—they'll *feel every step, strike, and breath like they were fighting right alongside it*.

Testing the Story's Emotional and Physical Balance

Every great martial arts story strikes a balance between two forces: the physical and the emotional. The kicks, throws, blocks, and battles thrill us—but it's the emotional stakes behind those moves that make them *matter*. Without a solid emotional core, the fights feel hollow. Without enough physical momentum, the story can drag. That's why, before your final draft is done, you need to test your story's *emotional and physical balance*—to ensure that every punch lands with purpose, and every quiet moment carries the weight of a clenched fist finally opening.

To begin, think of your story as a **heartbeat**. The physical scenes are the spikes—the sharp, sudden beats of tension and motion. The emotional scenes are the rests between—the places where your reader catches their breath, feels the bruise, and connects with your characters. Your job isn't to keep it all high energy, or all introspective, but to let the story rise and fall with natural rhythm. Like combat, it needs to flow.

Start your balance test by looking at **scene frequency**. Print out or list your chapters. Label them: action-heavy, emotional, both, or transitional. Do you see long stretches where nothing moves, or constant action with no time to feel? A strong martial arts story should have a steady alternation: fight, reflect, train, fall, rise. Action scenes should push your hero forward—but the emotional scenes should show *how those fights change them.*

You can also color-code your scenes—physically on paper or mentally in your outline. For example, red for fights or movement, blue for emotion or dialogue, yellow for philosophy or theme. Look at the pattern. If one color dominates, ask yourself: is the other side of the story being neglected? If your hero is fighting all the time but never showing fear, doubt, shame, or growth, the story might be exciting—but emotionally thin. If they're constantly brooding and rarely moving, the reader may lose that forward momentum.

Zoom in closer and check the **individual scenes**. Even a fight scene can have emotional balance. Is your protagonist just blocking and striking, or are they thinking, feeling, reacting internally? Are they fighting someone they care about, or someone who challenges their identity? What's at stake—just survival, or pride, or fear, or a vow? Conversely, in a quiet dialogue scene, are there *physical cues*? The tension of a clenched jaw, a foot shifting into a stance, a hand touching an old scar? This blending of emotion and motion makes even slow moments feel *alive.*

Ask ChatGPT to help with scene-level testing:

"Does this scene show emotional consequences after the fight?"

or

"Add physical detail to this emotional conversation so it feels grounded in a martial arts world."

Let your characters breathe—but also sweat. Let them cry—but also train. It's that blend that creates *truth.*

Another way to test balance is to follow your **character's body** through the story. Are they physically evolving alongside their emotional journey? In early chapters, maybe they move with hesitation or rage. By the end, are they fighting with clarity, control, and presence? Do their physical movements reflect inner transformation? If they've healed emotionally, it should show in how they walk, stand, breathe—even in silence.

Flip that and ask: *Are your emotional shifts triggered by physical moments?* A failed technique leads to shame. A sparring match brings back a painful memory. A fall during training forces them to finally admit they're afraid. When action causes emotion—and not just the other way around—you've got real depth.

If you're still unsure, give ChatGPT your story summary or a chapter and ask:

"Is there a good balance of physical action and emotional development in this section?"

or

"Where can I add emotional depth to support this fight scene?"

Don't overlook **thematic balance** either. If your story talks about discipline, inner peace, and growth, the action should reflect that. If the theme is rage and revenge, let the fights spiral with increasing violence—until something breaks. Let emotion and action reinforce each other, not pull in opposite directions.

Sometimes, imbalance is intentional. A story might open with pure physical chaos—fight after fight—and only later settle into emotional reflection. That's fine, as long as the shift feels *earned* and supported by character change. But if the story stays one-note throughout, you risk losing emotional power or physical intensity.

Think of the story like a martial artist in motion. The physical side is the stance, the movement, the strike. The emotional side is the breath, the presence, the reason *why* the strike is thrown. Without one, the other collapses.

So test the balance. Walk your story like a kata. Where are the hits? Where are the pauses? Where is the center?

Because when you blend the discipline of the body with the truth of the heart, the story doesn't just move—it *lives*. And every reader who walks that journey with you will feel it in their bones.

Creating Titles, Loglines, and Cover Blurbs That Sell

You've written your martial arts story. The battles are intense, the character arc is solid, the philosophy is sharp—but now it's time to package the story in a way that makes readers *want* to pick it up. That's where your title, logline, and cover blurb come in. These aren't just labels—they're promises. They tell potential readers what kind of experience they're in for, and whether that experience is worth their time. In a crowded market, a strong title and blurb can be the difference between getting noticed or getting skipped.

Let's start with the **title**. A great title is short, punchy, and packed with energy. It should capture either the tone, the theme, the setting, or the character. For a martial arts story, you want something that hints at *motion*, *struggle*, or *awakening*. Titles like *The Last Kata*, *Iron Circle*, *Shadow and Stance*, or *Fists of the Fallen* carry weight and clarity. They tell you that this is a story about more than just fights—it's about identity, honor, and transformation.

To brainstorm your title, ask yourself:

- What is the core theme of the story? (Redemption? Legacy? Control?)
- What's the unique visual or symbolic element? (A style, a setting, a myth?)
- What does the final confrontation *mean*?

You can combine these into a working structure. For example:

[Symbol or technique] + of + [theme or character trait] → *Strike of Honor*

[Character role] + in + [setting or metaphor] → *The Student in the Storm*

Or go minimalist and evocative: *Balance*, *Ashes*, *The Bow*

ChatGPT can help you brainstorm dozens of options fast. Try:

"Give me 20 martial arts story titles based on a tale of redemption and inner peace."

Next, let's look at the **logline**—a one- or two-sentence pitch that explains the core story hook. It should capture the protagonist, their challenge, and the stakes. Think of it like the first line in a trailer voiceover.

A good logline formula is:

When [protagonist] faces [problem/opponent], they must [action] before [consequence].

Example:

When a disgraced tournament champion is forced out of hiding to train a new generation of fighters, he must confront the ghosts of his past—or risk creating a legacy of destruction.

Or try a moodier one:

In a city where honor is currency and fists are law, one quiet fighter must break the rules to restore what was taken from him.

The goal of the logline is to make the reader lean in. You're not explaining the whole story—you're teasing its *soul*.

Now on to the **cover blurb**, the short paragraph on the back of your book or listing page. This is where you expand just enough to hook a reader fully. You want to introduce the main character, the central conflict, and the emotional pull—while keeping the pacing sharp.

Here's a breakdown for writing a strong blurb:

First sentence: Introduce the character and their situation.

Second sentence: Present the central conflict or what shakes their world.

Third sentence: Tease the rising stakes and internal struggle.

Final sentence: Close with a question or a sense of final choice.

Example:

He left the ring ten years ago. Now it's calling him back.

Kaito once stood at the top of the underground fight circuit—until a brutal betrayal forced him into exile. When a gifted but reckless student seeks him out, Kaito must confront everything he walked away from: the pain, the shame, and the rival who still fights in his shadow.

To survive the past, he must teach a new way forward. But in a world where mercy is weakness and pride kills, can he fight without becoming the monster he once was?

Let ChatGPT help tighten or expand your blurbs. You can prompt:

"Write a cover blurb for a martial arts story about a woman returning to her old dojo to face the rival who broke her spirit."

Then tweak the tone—make it more emotional, more mysterious, more cinematic—until it hits.

Also test your title, logline, and blurb by reading them aloud. Do they flow? Do they have *energy*? Do they sound like they belong on the back of a movie poster or book cover? That's the standard.

And finally—**make sure the tone matches the story**. If your story is gritty and violent, don't give it a poetic title that sounds like a fable. If your story is reflective and slow-burning, don't promise nonstop action. Readers pick up a story based on what it promises. If you deliver on that promise, they'll keep reading. If not, they'll walk away.

So treat your title like a stance. Your logline like a feint. And your blurb like a final strike.

Make them clean. Make them sharp. Make them *land*.

Building a Series around One Hero's Legacy

When a martial arts story ends with power and emotional resonance, it often leaves behind more than just a finished arc—it leaves behind a *legacy*. A legacy that can live on in sequels, spin-offs, or even entire sagas built around what the hero stood for, what they left behind, and who picks up the mantle next. Building a series around one hero's legacy doesn't mean repeating the same story with new villains. It means evolving the world, deepening the mythology, and exploring how one warrior's choices echo through the lives of others—sometimes for generations.

The key to designing a legacy-driven series is **thinking beyond the protagonist's arc**. Your original hero might have mastered their art, defeated their rival, or found inner peace—but what did that journey *change* in the world around them? Maybe they started a school. Maybe they wrote a book. Maybe they vanished, leaving behind a mystery or a trail of students, rivals, and enemies. That's where your next story begins—not with their fists, but with their *footprint*.

Start by deciding what the hero left behind—*physically, philosophically, emotionally*. It could be a fighting style that others now try to emulate or corrupt. A dojo that carries their teachings, or one that struggles under their absence. A child, a student, or a sworn enemy who never got closure. This is your foundation. A legacy isn't just what's remembered—it's what's *incomplete*.

If you want to build a series chronologically, the most natural approach is to follow the hero into a later stage of life—older, wiser, maybe broken, maybe revered. These stories explore *what it means to be a legend*. Do people expect too much? Have they twisted the hero's philosophy into something dangerous? Is the hero still capable of defending what they once stood for? These questions breathe new life into a familiar character by showing their evolution and the costs of their journey.

Or you might shift the spotlight entirely. Follow a **student or successor**. Someone who never met the hero but grew up idolizing their name. Or someone who trained under them but failed to understand their teachings until it was too late. This creates a natural tension between *what the hero stood for* and *what others think they stood for*. Legacy stories are rich with contrast—old truths misinterpreted, values distorted, ideals challenged.

The original hero's presence can remain strong, even if they're no longer on the page. Flashbacks, scrolls, teachings, rumors—every appearance should feel like a ripple from the original story. Let them shape events without dominating them. Let their absence create weight.

Another powerful technique is to show **multiple perspectives on the hero's legacy**. To one character, they were a saint. To another, a destroyer. To a third, a mystery. These perspectives add depth not only to the new characters, but to the original one. They remind the reader that no hero is ever one thing to all people.

As you develop the series, think about how the **martial arts itself evolves**. Does the hero's style fade into obscurity or evolve into something unrecognizable? Is it banned? Is it broken up into fragments and sought after like pieces of a sacred text? Is someone trying to revive it—and do they get it right? Legacy stories thrive on *interpretation versus intent*. Your new characters are trying to find meaning in something the original hero never meant to become legendary. That friction creates story.

You can also expand **the world itself**. Maybe the hero's final battle shook the political landscape. Maybe their teachings inspired rebellion. Maybe a rival school, once humbled, now dominates with a corrupted version of their style. A hero's legacy doesn't end with them—it spreads like a fire. And sometimes, it burns things they never meant to set ablaze.

ChatGPT can help you shape this kind of story quickly. Ask:

"Outline a series where each book follows a different martial artist influenced by a long-dead master whose teachings have been distorted."

or

"Write a summary of a martial arts story about the forgotten student of a once-famous warrior trying to rebuild their master's legacy."

Each entry in your series should carry a distinct emotional tone. One might be about reclaiming the truth. Another about escaping a shadow. Another about tearing down an old system. Let each book be its own test of *what the legacy really means*. And let each new protagonist fight with different intentions.

If your original hero ever reappears—aged, changed, or hidden—it should be *earned*. Their presence should shift the story like a thunderclap. A brief appearance can feel bigger than a full return. A single teaching passed down at the right moment can be more powerful than any physical comeback.

And finally, remember this: a legacy isn't a statue. It's *a living challenge*. Every book in your series should be about characters trying to define who they are *in the shadow of someone who came before*. Sometimes they'll live up to it. Sometimes they'll reject it. Sometimes they'll build something new entirely.

That's the power of a legacy story. The hero becomes more than a person. They become *the path*. And the next generation must decide: follow it, change it, or destroy it. Either way, the fight goes on.

Turning Your One-Day Draft Into a Book or Script

You've done it—you sat down, opened a blank page, and in one intense burst of inspiration and focus, you wrote your martial arts story in a day. That's no small feat. You've got your characters, your fights, your philosophy, your arc. But now comes the next step: *turning that one-day draft into something polished, professional, and publishable.* Whether you want to shape it into a novel or adapt it into a screenplay, the key is understanding that a first draft is *not* the finished product—it's the raw form of a powerful story waiting to be sculpted.

The first thing you should do is **step back for a moment**. Let the draft sit for a day or two. This isn't just about rest—it's about clearing your mind so you can come back with fresh eyes. When you return, don't judge the draft too harshly. Think of it like a training montage captured in real time—messy, intense, full of raw energy. Your job now is to shape it, not erase it.

Start with **structure review**. Whether you're turning your story into a novel or a screenplay, you need to make sure the beats hit in the right places. Does the story open with a hook? Does the protagonist face a clear challenge? Is there a midpoint shift, an emotional low point, and a final confrontation that brings everything full circle? Even if you were writing fast, most stories instinctively find their way toward these shapes—but now you can sharpen them.

Use ChatGPT to help clarify that shape:

"Break this story into three acts and identify the major turning points."

or

"Help outline the emotional and physical journey of this martial arts protagonist across the story."

This gives you a map to work with as you begin to revise.

If your goal is a **book**, your next step is expanding and refining the prose. One-day drafts are often fast on dialogue and action but light on setting, emotion, and internal reflection. Read through and ask:

- Can the reader feel the environment?
- Are the character's emotions clear during action scenes?
- Are there moments where the pacing needs to slow down so the reader can catch their breath?

Add richness where needed. A dojo isn't just a room—it's the scent of sweat and cedar, the sound of bare feet on wood. A fight isn't just blows—it's memory, fear, pride, doubt. Let the reader *feel* what the characters feel.

If your goal is a **script**, the focus shifts to clarity, visuals, and dialogue. You'll want to reformat the draft into screenplay style (using software like Final Draft, Celtx, or free tools like Arc Studio). Focus on *what can be seen and heard.* Internal thoughts must become action or dialogue. Describe movement economically, and make sure each scene change drives the story forward.

Ask ChatGPT:

"Convert this chapter into screenplay format using proper scene headings and dialogue style."

Or:

"Rewrite this internal monologue as visual cues and action beats for a martial arts film."

Also, in both formats, check for **consistency**. One-day drafts sometimes include details that change halfway through—names, timelines, fight outcomes. Go back and make sure the character arcs are smooth, the world logic holds, and the style is cohesive from start to finish.

Once that's done, focus on **rhythm and pacing**. A book needs to vary its tempo—action, dialogue, reflection. A script needs clear scene transitions and compelling act breaks. Wherever the pace drags or rushes, adjust. Maybe a fight is too long without stakes. Maybe a quiet scene doesn't build tension the way it should. Think of this process as refining a kata—cleaning the form until every movement feels intentional.

Now bring in a **test reader or listener**—even just one. If you're writing a novel, ask them where they got bored, confused, or deeply invested. If it's a script, do a table read with friends or read it out loud yourself. You'll immediately hear what's flat and what sings.

And finally, title it, format it, and **package it with purpose**. If it's a book, write your blurb and start researching publishing paths—indie or traditional. If it's a script, write your logline and short pitch, and start looking at screenwriting contests, pitch sessions, or indie production routes.

Remember: your one-day draft is not the rough version of your story—it's the *spine*. The soul is already there. You just have to give it the body to match.

Because a great martial arts story doesn't just throw punches—it *lands*. And now, your job is to shape every scene, every moment, every line until the final version *hits with purpose*.

You already wrote the fight. Now you finish the form.

Marketing and Sharing Your Martial Arts Tale

You've written your martial arts story, shaped it, polished it, and now it's time to step out of the dojo and into the marketplace. Whether your story is a self-published novel, a short film script, a web series pilot, or even an illustrated graphic novel, marketing isn't about selling out—it's about *inviting others into the world you built*. Your job now is to honor the story you've created by getting it into the hands of people who will love it. And in the spirit of martial arts, marketing should be approached with discipline, strategy, and intention.

Start with your **audience**. Martial arts fans are incredibly diverse. Some are lifelong practitioners. Others are obsessed with action films, anime, or classic kung fu cinema. Some love gritty modern tales, others love philosophical journeys or fantasy-inspired fights. Know who your story speaks to. Is it for fans of *The Karate Kid*, *Ip Man*, *Avatar: The Last Airbender*, *Warrior*, or *Cobra Kai*? Each of these references a different audience vibe. Your marketing should align with that energy.

Begin by creating a **one-sentence hook**—the essence of your story that's easy to say, remember, and share. Something like:

"A disgraced martial arts prodigy must train the rival who ruined his life to stop a greater threat."

This becomes your pitch line, your social media caption, your video intro. If your story was a trailer, this is the voiceover line that grabs attention.

Then build a **platform**. This doesn't mean you have to become a full-time influencer—but you do need a central hub where readers or viewers can find your work. A basic website or landing page, an Instagram or TikTok account, or a YouTube channel if you're visually inclined. Use these spaces to share your journey:

- Behind-the-scenes writing or training posts
- Short clips or teasers from your story if you're filming it
- Martial arts philosophy quotes that reflect your theme
- Character art, fan casting ideas, or soundtrack inspiration
- Clips of you reading key scenes aloud or discussing your hero's journey

Let the audience connect not just with the story—but with your *passion*. That's what builds trust and interest.

Don't underestimate the power of **visuals**. Even if your project is a novel, create or commission artwork. A dynamic cover, character sketch, or stylized poster can stop a scroll on social media way faster than a block of text. You can use ChatGPT and image-generation tools together to produce concept images for your world. Share those alongside short, powerful lines from your story.

If your story is available online (Amazon, Wattpad, Webtoon, etc.), make sure you have a **strong blurb and an eye-catching title**. Use keywords that martial arts fans search for: *dojo*, *master*, *honor*, *rival*, *fury*, *shadow*, *dragon*, *path*, *iron*, *fist*, *discipline*, *legacy*. These signal genre and mood instantly.

Join **communities that care**. Martial arts forums, writing groups, action film fan pages, martial arts subreddits, Discord writing servers—these places are full of readers who want new stories with heart and movement. Don't just drop links—participate. Talk about your favorite fight scenes in film. Ask others about their martial arts journeys. When you share your own work later, it feels organic—and people are more likely to support someone they've connected with.

You can also reach out to **book bloggers**, **script reviewers**, or **martial arts podcasters**. Offer a free copy, or ask if they'd like to interview you about writing a martial arts story. Even a single feature can create a ripple effect, especially if the right people see it.

For film scripts or indie shorts, consider entering **script competitions or film festivals** that love action and genre work. Look at:

- Screencraft's Action & Adventure Contest
- The Martial Arts Film Festival (yes, it exists!)
- Shore Scripts
- ISA's Fast Track
- Raindance, Slamdance, and smaller regional festivals
  Having "Finalist" or "Official Selection" on your project's page adds a layer of credibility and discoverability.

Let ChatGPT help you create all your promo materials:

"Write five tweet-sized pitches for a martial arts story about a teacher seeking redemption through one last student."

or

"Give me a short blurb for a martial arts fantasy novel about a hidden style passed through dreams."

And don't forget the **power of collaboration**. Team up with martial arts instructors, YouTube reviewers, or fitness influencers. Maybe someone would demo a form from your story. Maybe they'd read a scene aloud. Now your story is moving beyond the page—and into *practice*.

Ultimately, marketing your martial arts tale is just another version of the story's message: *share your truth with courage*. Step into the arena. Bow with humility. Then show the world what your story can do.

Because somewhere out there, a reader or viewer is waiting for exactly what you've written.

They just don't know it yet. So go tell them.

Training for the Next One: Becoming a Martial Arts Story Machine

Finishing a martial arts story is a victory. Maybe even a masterpiece. But what if you don't want to stop at one? What if this was just the beginning of something greater? A way of life. A rhythm. A creative discipline that flows as naturally as breath in a kata. You've told one story—but now it's time to *train for the next*. Because just like in martial arts, storytelling sharpens through repetition, reflection, and a commitment to the path. This is how you become a martial arts story machine—not by forcing it, but by *living the process*.

The first shift is mental. Stop thinking of the story as an event. Think of it as *practice*. One story isn't the peak. It's the rep. The drill. The sparring match. The beautiful part? The more you write, the more you *feel* what works—the flow of a scene, the heartbeat of a character, the moment when action meets meaning. The goal isn't perfection every time. The goal is presence. Showing up to the story again and again until it flows through you.

Start by creating a **routine that feels like training.** That could be writing 500 words every morning, brainstorming story ideas once a week, or drafting a short film script every month. It's not about quantity alone—it's about rhythm. When your writing becomes a practice, your mind starts building stories even when you're not at the keyboard. Fights start choreographing themselves in your head. Character arcs unfold during your walks. You're not forcing stories. You're *living in story mode*.

Set small goals that lead to big momentum. One flash fiction piece. One short story in a new subgenre. One logline a day for a week. You'll build a library of ideas that you can pull from anytime—just like a martial artist switches stances mid-fight. Keep a "dojo notebook" or digital file where you store every cool character name, thematic idea, or striking setting that pops into your mind. These fragments will become the building blocks of your next tale.

Use ChatGPT as part of your process—not just when you're stuck, but as part of your *creative training regimen*. Set up daily prompts like:

"Give me three martial arts story ideas with a twist ending."

"Create a rival character whose style reflects their obsession with control."

"Outline a redemption arc for a disgraced monk forced back into violence."

Think of it like a kata—repeated drills to build reflexes. Over time, the responses will sharpen your instincts. You'll see patterns. You'll remix elements naturally. You'll feel what's missing and what hits hard.

It also helps to develop your own *style signature*. Maybe you love stories set in modern urban cities with spiritual undertones. Maybe you lean into fantasy duels with mythical weapons. Maybe your characters always struggle with mercy. Whatever your personal flavor is, lean into it. Let it evolve, but own it. That signature becomes the thread that ties all your stories together—even if each one stands alone.

Take breaks between stories—but don't disconnect. In that rest time, study what inspires you. Watch classic martial arts films. Read graphic novels. Train physically if you can. Take a walk and watch how people move. Every breath of inspiration becomes fuel for the next strike of the keyboard. Your stories become layered not just with action—but with *lived experience and curiosity*.

Set a goal to always be in one of three modes: *generating, drafting, or refining*. Generating means you're exploring ideas, writing loglines, developing characters. Drafting means you're in the zone, writing your next story. Refining means you're editing, shaping, or prepping a piece for publication or performance. That way, you're always moving. Always engaged. Always leveling up.

And here's the truth: the more stories you write, the more *fluid* it all becomes. Plotting becomes instinctive. Emotional arcs start writing themselves. You know how to pace a fight. You feel where to insert that moment of silence before the final blow. Your first drafts get tighter. Your edits get faster. You're not just writing stories—you're mastering the form.

Share your work often. Get feedback. Teach others. Collaborate. Build a community of fellow writers and martial arts fans. The more you engage with others, the more your voice grows—and the more energy you'll have to keep going. The dojo isn't a lonely place when it's filled with people on the same path.

So yes, celebrate your completed story. But more importantly—*step back into the circle*. Bow. Breathe. Begin again.

Because mastery doesn't come from writing one story. It comes from making storytelling your practice. From honoring the form, sharpening your technique, and pouring yourself into each new fight on the page.

You're not done.

You're just getting started.

Examples of Prompts for Martial Arts Story Design and Structure

A strong martial arts story often starts with a strong *prompt*—a spark that sets the whole journey in motion. Whether you're writing a novel, screenplay, short story, or just brainstorming ideas, using clear, focused prompts helps guide your creativity with purpose. The right prompt doesn't just hand you a plot—it sets up structure, character arc, theme, tone, and world-building all at once.

Here are examples of well-crafted prompts you can use or adapt, broken down into categories that touch on story *design*, *structure*, and *narrative clarity*:

Story Concept and Core Conflict

- "Create a martial arts story where a fighter returns to their hometown to face the master who once expelled them from the dojo."
- "Write a martial arts story set in a future where physical combat is outlawed, and underground dojos preserve forbidden techniques."
- "Describe a story about a peaceful monk forced back into combat when an old student returns as a warlord."
- "Give me a story idea where a fighter must choose between winning a tournament and saving a friend's life."

These prompts create an immediate setup and conflict that leads directly to a structured arc: origin, challenge, turning point, moral choice, and climax.

Hero's Journey Structure

- "Outline a martial arts story where a reluctant fighter refuses the call to train, but is forced into battle after a tragedy strikes their family."
- "Design a three-act story where the protagonist begins as a brash street brawler and slowly learns inner discipline from an unlikely mentor."
- "Build a hero's journey in a martial arts setting where each act is tied to mastering a different element: Earth (foundation), Water (adaptability), and Fire (intensity)."

These guide you through familiar structure while giving the emotional and thematic milestones needed to track a character's growth.

Character-Driven Structure Prompts

- "Create a story where a blind martial artist must rely on instinct and sound to defeat opponents who underestimate them."
- "Write about a fighter who has never lost but begins to unravel emotionally when faced with a worthy opponent who refuses to quit."
- "Design a story where the protagonist is training to defeat a villain—only to find out they're siblings separated at birth."

These prompts help you align *story beats* with *character revelations*, ensuring the structure grows out of internal struggle.

Philosophy and Thematic Prompts

- "Write a martial arts story that explores the theme of restraint versus power, with the final conflict resolved through mercy, not violence."
- "Give me a story outline where the protagonist's style is based on deception and trickery—and they must learn to fight with honesty to win."
- "Create a narrative where the antagonist believes fear builds strength, and the protagonist must prove that strength comes from peace."

These will naturally lead to stories structured around debate, personal transformation, and a final philosophical confrontation.

World and Setting-Based Structure

- "Describe a martial arts story set in a city divided into five fighting schools, each representing a different virtue. The protagonist must master all five styles to unify the city."
- "Create a story where the last practitioner of an ancient martial art lives alone in the mountains, and must pass on their knowledge before their time runs out."
- "Write a martial arts fantasy where the spiritual energy of the land is tied to fighters' emotions—and the villain seeks to corrupt the balance by triggering rage."

These give you both a setting *and* a story structure: Act I introduces the world and its rules, Act II breaks those rules, and Act III either restores or reshapes them.

Tournament and Progression-Based Story Prompts

- "Outline a martial arts story where a new student must climb through a ranked system of fighters, each representing a different weakness in their own character."
- "Write a tournament arc where the protagonist keeps winning but starts to lose themselves emotionally—until one unexpected fight breaks the cycle."
- "Give me a martial arts series structure where each episode focuses on a new challenger who teaches the hero a different lesson."

These naturally lend themselves to episodic structure or progression-based arcs with mini-climaxes and layered growth.

Dual Narrative or Rival-Based Structure Prompts

- "Create a story told from the perspectives of two fighters who trained together, separated over ideology, and are destined to meet again."
- "Write a martial arts tale where the antagonist's rise to power is shown in parallel to the protagonist's fall from grace—and they cross paths at the final battle."
- "Give me a story where the 'villain' is revealed to have been protecting the same ideal as the hero—but through different means."

These prompts set up a structure that uses *mirroring* and *intersection*, leading to powerful, character-driven climaxes.

Once you've selected or created a prompt, you can follow up with ChatGPT to build out the structure:

- "Based on this idea, outline the story in three acts."
- "What's the midpoint twist in this story?"
- "How does the character change emotionally from the start to the end?"
- "What internal flaw must the protagonist overcome during the climax?"

By combining strong initial prompts with structural follow-ups, you're not just generating story ideas—you're laying the foundation for compelling, complete narratives.

In the end, a great martial arts story doesn't just showcase fights. It showcases *transformation through challenge*—and prompts like these help you design stories where every block, strike, and step leads to a deeper truth.

Examples of Prompts for Designing Compelling Martial Arts Characters

A compelling martial arts character doesn't just throw punches—they carry wounds, beliefs, discipline, and fire. Whether they're a bruised brawler in an alleyway, a graceful monk who fights like poetry, or a quiet teen who trains in secret after school, every martial arts protagonist, rival, master, or villain needs emotional depth and fighting purpose. You want readers or viewers to remember *who* this person is—not just what they do with their fists.

Great character creation starts with great prompts. Prompts that go beyond surface traits and dig into personality, philosophy, training history, emotional baggage, and internal contradiction. Let's explore examples you can use to shape fighters who are memorable, multi-dimensional, and story-ready.

Identity and Backstory Prompts

- "Create a martial artist who once trained to protect others but walked away after failing to save someone they loved."
- "Design a character who was raised in a family that forbade violence, but secretly trains in martial arts to feel in control of their emotions."
- "Give me a fighter who was trained from birth in a legendary style they now believe is fundamentally flawed."
- "Invent a character who fights not because they want to win, but because they fear what happens if they don't."

These prompts focus on *why* they fight, not just *how* they fight—key for emotional resonance.

Style Reflects Personality Prompts

- "Create a martial artist whose fighting style is based on rhythm and improvisation, matching their unpredictable and rebellious personality."
- "Design a character who uses a soft, evasive style because they can't bear to hurt others—even when fighting for their life."
- "Describe a fighter whose rigid, traditional form mirrors their need for control and fear of emotional vulnerability."
- "Give me a character who disguises brutal, aggressive techniques with a calm and meditative outward presence."

These push you to design characters where *the body tells the story*.

Flaws, Contradictions, and Internal Conflict Prompts

- "Invent a martial artist who teaches peace but secretly craves the chaos of combat."
- "Create a fighter who is terrified of losing but refuses to train with anyone better than them."
- "Write about a character whose loyalty to their master blinds them to that master's dark past."
- "Design a student who wants to abandon violence but is the only one who can stop a coming war."

These lead to tension and growth—fuel for character arcs.

Relationships and Rivalries Prompts

- "Design two martial arts characters: one who believes in winning at all costs, and one who believes that victory without honor is defeat."
- "Create a fighter whose style is built to counter their former best friend's—after the two fell out during a tournament years ago."
- "Write about a character who never beat their master in sparring—and now must fight them for real."
- "Describe a student who must train under their family's worst enemy to survive."

Rivalries deepen motivation and raise stakes. Use them to layer emotional meaning into conflict.

Training and Transformation Prompts

- "Give me a martial arts character who begins as an arrogant champion and slowly unlearns everything to rebuild their foundation."
- "Create a fighter who has been training in solitude and must now learn to fight *with* a team for the first time."
- "Describe a character who can mimic any technique they see—but still feels like they don't have a style of their own."
- "Write about a student who discovers their greatest strength after failing every formal test in their dojo."

These are perfect for tracking long-term arcs across a series or film.

Cultural and World-Building-Driven Prompts

- "Invent a martial artist whose fighting style is inspired by the wind patterns of their mountainous homeland."
- "Design a character who comes from a culture where martial arts are sacred rituals, not sport."
- "Create a fighter trained by a secretive society that considers emotion a weakness—but who fights with unrestrained passion."
- "Write about a character whose martial arts style is banned in the modern world, forcing them to hide or adapt."

These prompts let you tie *character design* directly to *setting, tradition, and lore.*

Emotion in Combat Prompts

- "Describe a martial artist who loses control when angry—and must learn to fight with love instead of rage."
- "Create a fighter who never lands the first strike because they believe violence should only be reactive."
- "Write about a warrior who discovers they fight best when protecting someone else."
- "Design a martial artist who cannot fight without reliving trauma—until they find a reason bigger than pain."

These will help you design fights that are *emotional conversations*, not just physical sequences.

Once you've chosen a prompt, you can follow up with ChatGPT using:

- "Build a full character profile based on this prompt."
- "Describe how this character changes emotionally and physically over the course of a three-act story."
- "What kind of opponent would challenge this character's philosophy the most?"

By stacking prompts like these with deeper exploration, you'll create fighters who *live and breathe* on the page or screen. Characters whose battles aren't just about technique—but about belief, fear, love, memory, and transformation.

Because in martial arts fiction, every character should fight like no one else—because no one else carries *their story*.

Examples of Prompts for Martial Arts World Building

World-building in martial arts fiction goes far beyond designing a dojo or naming a technique. It's about crafting a society, a philosophy, a rhythm to life where martial arts isn't just a skill—it's a language, a religion, a rebellion, a secret, or a cultural cornerstone. Whether your story takes place in a hyper-realistic urban underground, a mystical mountain society, or a post-apocalyptic wasteland where combat is law, the richness of your world makes every strike and stance feel earned.

And the best way to build that world? With sharp, focused prompts. Prompts that unlock history, hierarchy, cultural depth, and environmental tension—all while staying true to the spirit of martial arts.

Here are some powerful prompt categories you can use to design unique, immersive martial arts worlds.

Cultural and Philosophical Foundations

- "Create a society where martial arts is not taught—it's inherited. What does that mean for someone born outside the tradition who wants to learn?"
- "Design a world where each region practices a different martial art based on its surrounding terrain and philosophy—what tensions arise when those regions clash?"
- "Write about a civilization where martial arts rituals replace political elections."
- "Imagine a society where combat is a sacred act and fights must be witnessed by a spiritual elder to be considered valid."

These prompts help define the cultural *weight* of martial arts in your setting—whether it's spiritual, social, or survival-based.

Dojo, Clan, or School Systems

- "Design three rival martial arts schools, each based on a different animal philosophy—one emphasizes speed, one patience, one deception."
- "Create a martial arts hierarchy where style advancement is determined not by technique, but by mental clarity and community service."
- "Write about a secret martial arts order that has infiltrated all levels of government—but only reveals its presence to those who defeat one of its masters."
- "Invent a setting where dojos are mobile—caravans that travel from town to town, teaching and challenging local fighters."

This gives structure to your world's organizations and how martial arts groups interact with the public and each other.

Law, Conflict, and Power

- "Build a world where martial arts is the only legal form of conflict resolution, and fighters serve as mobile judges."
- "Design a city-state ruled by former tournament champions. What kind of justice, economy, and politics come from a system built on combat?"
- "Imagine a world where martial arts has been outlawed—what happens to those who still practice in secret?"

- "Create a futuristic world where martial artists are hired as diplomats, spies, and negotiators because of their controlled discipline and trained focus."

Use these prompts to explore how martial arts shapes law enforcement, rebellion, diplomacy, and societal rules.

Training and Environment

- "Describe how a desert region trains its martial artists to fight with limited visibility, heat, and dehydration."
- "Create a mountainous monastery where each level of elevation represents a new stage of mastery."
- "Invent a rainforest dojo where fighters learn to move in silence to avoid alerting predators."
- "Write about a floating city where martial artists train on constantly moving platforms, learning balance above all."

Environmental conditions add flavor to the style, form, and mindset of your characters—and can create unique challenges during fights.

Tournaments, Rituals, and Combat Culture

- "Design a tournament that takes place once every decade and determines the spiritual balance of the world."
- "Write about a coming-of-age ceremony where a fighter must spar with a spirit representing their inner weakness."
- "Invent a public duel ritual where the loser must take a vow of silence until they win their next match."
- "Describe a combat culture where pain is seen as purification and fighters mark their skin with the number of times they've lost."

These prompts build cultural stakes around combat and make every fight more meaningful than just survival or victory.

Weapons, Techniques, and Forbidden Knowledge

- "Create a lost martial art that was banned because it blurred the line between healing and killing."
- "Design a sacred weapon that only activates in battle when the wielder's mind is perfectly still."
- "Imagine a martial arts style that manipulates sound or breath instead of strikes."
- "Write about an underground archive of forbidden scrolls, each containing a style designed to counter a specific philosophy."

Martial arts worlds often revolve around what knowledge is passed on, what's hidden, and what's feared. These prompts help you explore that.

Modern and Futuristic Martial Worlds

- "Design a near-future city where martial arts tournaments are globally televised—and corporate sponsors control the fighters."
- "Create a cyberpunk dojo that uses augmented reality to train against AI-generated opponents who evolve with each match."
- "Write about a digital martial arts archive that uploads fighting styles directly into the mind—but only temporarily."

- “Imagine a post-apocalyptic world where martial artists preserve civilization through discipline, story, and self-defense.”

Blending martial arts with sci-fi or modern settings gives you exciting contrasts between ancient values and futuristic tools.

Once you have a solid world-building idea, you can refine it further with follow-up prompts like:

- “What kind of conflict would naturally arise in this society?”
- “What moral dilemmas would a fighter face in this world?”
- “How does this environment shape the protagonist’s emotional growth?”
- “What does honor look like here—and who breaks it?”

A well-built martial arts world doesn’t just support your story—it *tests your characters*. It pushes them to question who they are, why they fight, and what kind of strength really matters.

Because in martial arts fiction, the world isn’t just a stage. It’s the *second opponent*—and the best ones make your hero stronger every time they get knocked down.

Examples of Prompts for Martial Arts Story Ideas

When you're ready to write your next martial arts story but staring at a blank page, what you need is a spark. A great story idea prompt can ignite the entire narrative—from protagonist to conflict to setting—with just a few powerful lines. Whether you want something grounded and realistic, mythical and magical, or dystopian and futuristic, prompts can help you leap over hesitation and into action. The key is asking the right kind of question that pushes character, stakes, and style all at once.

Here are a range of creative, layered, and thought-provoking prompts to inspire your next martial arts tale.

Classic but Character-Driven Story Ideas

- *A young fighter enters a tournament to prove themselves but discovers their strongest opponent is their own sibling, hidden behind a mask.*
- *A former champion now works as a janitor at a dojo—until the arrival of a student who unknowingly resurrects their buried past.*
- *An aging martial artist begins to lose their reflexes just as an old enemy resurfaces, demanding a final match to settle a decades-old score.*
- *A student trains in secret after their family forbids violence—but is forced to reveal their skill to protect someone they love.*

These ideas hit on core emotional arcs: redemption, secrecy, legacy, and inner conflict—all grounded in martial arts structure.

Philosophical and Thematic Prompts

- *A fighter who has never been defeated begins to lose on purpose to understand the meaning of failure.*
- *A peaceful monk is challenged to a duel by a violent prodigy, but refuses to fight—forcing a battle of wills instead of fists.*
- *A tournament is held where fighters are judged not only on technique, but on intention—and only those with pure purpose may advance.*
- *A martial artist must decide whether to teach a forbidden technique to save a village, knowing it could unleash greater violence.*

These prompts ask questions about identity, ethics, restraint, and what it *means* to fight—perfect for emotionally layered stories.

High-Concept and Speculative Story Ideas

- *In a world where memories can be stolen through physical touch, a martial artist uses forgotten techniques to reclaim what was lost.*
- *After a global blackout renders all weapons useless, only hand-to-hand martial arts can maintain peace and order.*
- *A warrior is born into a society where martial skills are passed down genetically, but they are born without any—but still choose to fight.*
- *A time-traveling martial artist must learn ancient techniques from various eras to survive a centuries-spanning*

war of styles.

These are perfect for graphic novels, short films, or serialized fiction that blends genre with tradition.

Tournament and Rivalry-Based Ideas

- *A disgraced fighter enters a secret underground tournament where each opponent represents a different regret from their past.*
- *Two childhood friends who trained under the same master now lead rival schools—one preaching control, the other, freedom.*
- *A global martial arts competition has been rigged by a powerful corporate sponsor—until one unranked wildcard starts winning.*
- *A mysterious tournament only opens to those who have suffered a personal loss—and no one knows who created it or why.*

Rivalries and competitions provide natural structure for action, pacing, and emotional payoff—ideal for novel series or screenplays.

Villain-Centered Prompts

- *A villain once defeated in their youth returns as a revered master—and only the hero knows the truth of their past.*
- *A martial arts cult rises, promising spiritual awakening through combat—but its leader has dark plans for the most powerful fighters.*
- *A former student, cast out for breaking the code, begins targeting their old dojo's members one by one.*
- *A warlord builds an army of martial artists by stealing and blending forbidden techniques from every known style.*

Flipping the narrative toward the antagonist or shadow side of martial arts adds danger, depth, and strong external stakes.

Mystical or Fantasy Martial Arts Ideas

- *A hidden temple in the mountains teaches a martial art passed down by elemental spirits—each student bonds to one.*
- *A sacred scroll teaches the "final technique"—but no one knows what it does, only that it must never be used.*
- *A fighter is chosen by an ancient weapon that requires a duel every full moon to remain bonded to its wielder.*
- *A student's dreams are haunted by visions of a master they've never met—until they discover the dreams are memories from a past life.*

These work beautifully in animated stories, martial fantasy novels, or hybrid genres where magic enhances the fight.

Low-Budget or Indie Film-Friendly Prompts

- *A delivery driver uses their childhood martial arts training to fight back against a local gang threatening their neighborhood.*
- *A martial arts instructor opens a free dojo in a poor district, but an old rival's students start sabotaging the school.*
- *A single-location story: Two martial artists trapped in a warehouse must work together to escape, but only one can*

leave with the scroll.

- *A minimalist story about a fighter who wanders from town to town, settling local disputes with a single, peaceful strike.*

These are tight, affordable concepts that still carry weight, emotion, and potential for high-impact storytelling.

Once you find a prompt that excites you, use ChatGPT to build it out:

- "Outline this story in three acts."
- "Describe the main character and their emotional arc."
- "Generate a list of scenes where the fights represent key psychological turning points."

And don't be afraid to remix. Combine prompts. Flip the hero and villain. Change the setting. Ask "What if...?" over and over until it becomes your own.

Because in martial arts storytelling, the first idea is the opening stance—but the real story begins with the *next move.*

Your One-Day Martial Arts Writing Game Plan – From Start to Publish

You don't need weeks or months to write a powerful martial arts story. With the right mindset, structure, and tools—including ChatGPT—you can go from idea to finished piece in a single day. The key is staying focused, writing with purpose, and allowing structure to guide your creativity instead of slow it down. This chapter gives you a practical, step-by-step game plan to write your martial arts story—from a blank page to something you can share, publish, or even produce.

Let's break your writing day into five focused phases:

Hour 1: Start with the Core – Idea, Conflict, and Character

Begin by choosing one compelling prompt to work from. If you don't have one, use ChatGPT to help:

"Give me three martial arts story prompts that feature a redemption arc, a personal rivalry, and a unique fighting style."

Once you pick your idea, quickly define:

- **Protagonist:** Who are they? What do they want? Why do they fight?
- **Conflict:** What are they up against? Who challenges them physically or emotionally?
- **Climax:** What's the final fight or test? How does it reflect their internal growth?

Write this out as a few sentences. Don't overthink. You're laying a foundation.

Hours 2–4: Write the First Draft – Three Acts, One Flow

Structure your story in three acts:

- **Act I (Beginning):** Set the stage. Introduce your fighter, their world, their flaw, and the first sign of conflict. End with a moment that pushes them into training or a deeper challenge.
- **Act II (Middle):** Training, conflict, emotional resistance. This is where they grow, stumble, and face the rival or obstacle that represents their inner weakness. Include at least one memorable fight or dramatic test.
- **Act III (End):** The final showdown. The character now applies what they've learned—not just with fists, but with wisdom. Win or lose, the emotional arc completes.

Write fast. Don't edit. If you stall, ask ChatGPT:

"Write a training montage scene where the hero is pushed beyond their limits emotionally and physically."

Or:

"Describe a fight where the hero is forced to use a lesson they rejected earlier."

Let the momentum carry you. Trust the process.

Hour 5: Edit for Flow and Emotional Punch

Take a short break, then come back and read your draft aloud. Listen for:

- **Flow:** Do scenes transition smoothly? Are there abrupt or unclear moments?
- **Emotion:** Do you *feel* the character's growth? Do the fights carry meaning?
- **Clarity:** Cut unnecessary lines. Add a few vivid details if needed.

You can ask ChatGPT:

"Tighten this fight scene for pacing while keeping the emotion intact."

or

"Rewrite this ending to feel more like an earned emotional victory."

Don't aim for perfection—aim for clarity and *impact.*

Hour 6: Create the Title, Blurb, and Final Line

Now give your story the final polish:

- **Title:** Choose something powerful that reflects theme or tone.
  Try prompts like:

"Give me ten martial arts story titles about legacy, redemption, and discipline."

- **Blurb:** One paragraph that introduces the hero, the conflict, and the emotional stakes.
  Ask:

"Write a compelling back cover blurb for a martial arts novella about a fallen master training one last student."

- **Final Line:** Make it clean and emotional. A breath. A bow. A final choice.
  Ask ChatGPT to help shape it:

"Give me five poetic last lines for a martial arts story about finding peace through restraint."

These finishing touches will make your story feel complete and ready to share.

Hour 7: Format, Package, and Publish

Depending on your format:

- **For a short story or novella:** Save it as a PDF or ePub. Use formatting tools like Reedsy or Draft2Digital to clean it up.
- **For a script:** Format with tools like Arc Studio, Celtx, or WriterDuet.
- **For sharing online:** Publish to platforms like: Draft2Digital, Wattpad, Medium, or Substack. Include your title, blurb, and a simple cover image (which you can generate with AI tools).

If you want to self-publish on Kindle, ChatGPT can guide you:

"Give me a checklist for uploading my short martial arts book to Amazon KDP."

Don't wait for perfection. Just *publish*. You can revise or expand later.

Bonus: Share and Reflect

After publishing, tell the story behind the story. Post your blurb and title on social media with a line like:

"Wrote a martial arts story in one day using ChatGPT—and I'm proud of it. Here's the link."

Then take 5 minutes to reflect:

- What worked?
- What surprised you?
- What would you do differently next time?

This closes the loop and opens the door to your *next story*.

Final Thoughts

Writing a martial arts story in one day is not about rushing—it's about entering a creative flow with discipline, structure, and heart. With ChatGPT in your corner, you're never writing alone. You're sparring with ideas, refining your instincts, and mastering the art of storytelling one breath at a time.

Remember: the first story is the warm-up. The next one is your next strike. So bow. Breathe. And begin again.

I hope you found inspiration within these pages. If you liked this book, please leave a review where you bought it. Thank you from the author.

www.ingramcontent.com/pod-product-compliance
Lightning Source LLC
LaVergne TN
LVHW082348200926
848481LV00012B/3490